W9-DEX-200

THE CURSE™

AN ONI PRESS PUBLICATION

THE CUR

WRITTEN & ILLUSTRATED BY

DESIGNED BY

COLLECTION EDITED BY

COVER BY

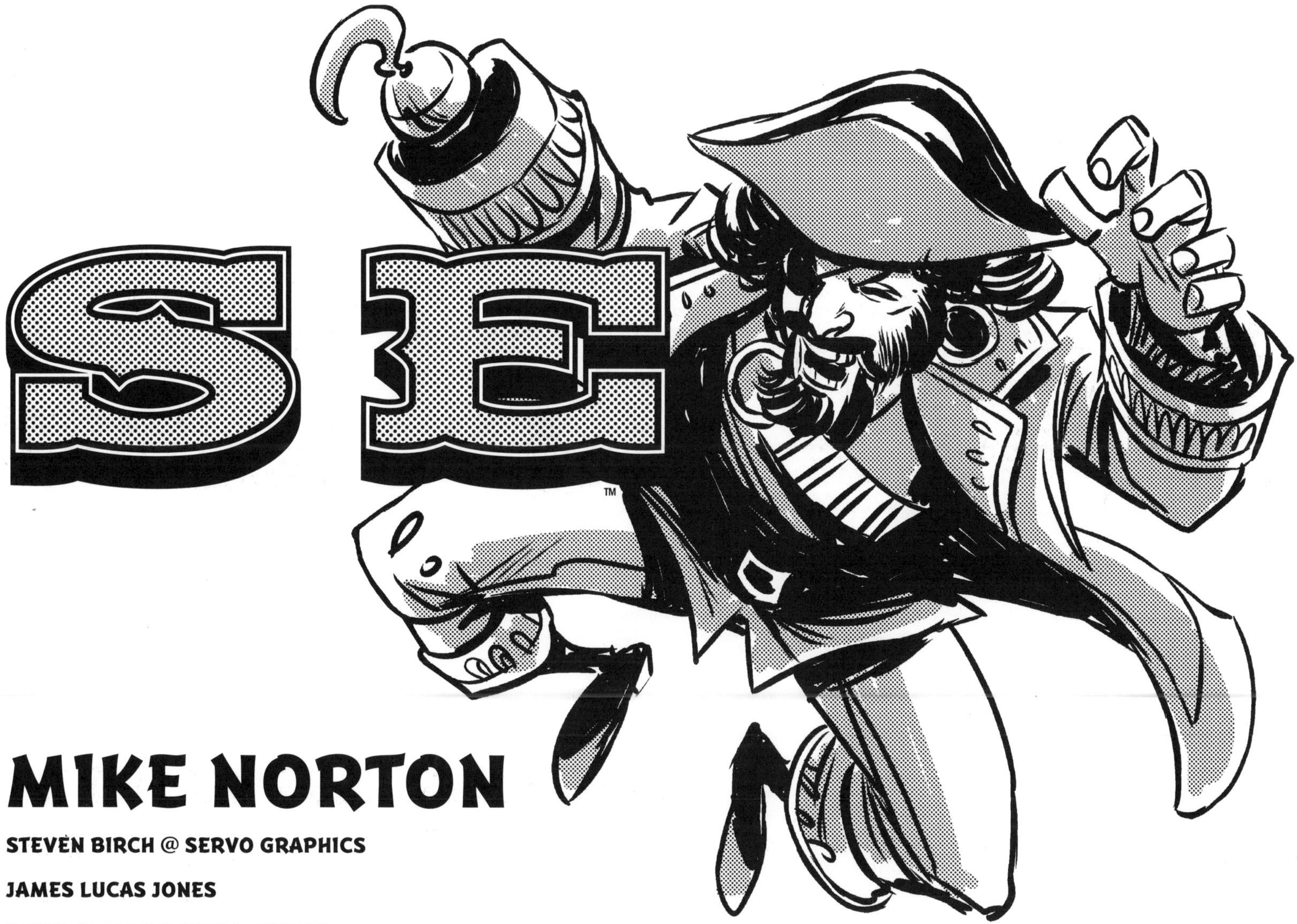

MIKE NORTON

STEVEN BIRCH @ SERVO GRAPHICS

JAMES LUCAS JONES

DAVID "LOOPY DAVE" DUNSTAN

Hardcover design by Troy Look

Oni Press, Inc.
Joe Nozemack, publisher
James Lucas Jones, editor in chief
George Rohac, operations director
Keith Wood, art director
Tom Shimmin, marketing coordinator
Amber LaPraim, marketing coordinator
Jill Beaton, editor
Charlie Chu, editor
Troy Look, digital prepress lead

onipress.com
ihatemike.com

First edition: October 2012

ISBN 978-1-934964-88-0

Library of Congress Control Number: 2012930898

10 9 8 7 6 5 4 3 2 1

Mike Norton's The Curse, August 2012. Published by Oni Press, Inc., 1305 SE Martin Luther King Jr. Blvd., Suite A, Portland, OR 97214.

PRINTED IN CHINA

INTRODUCTION

This book? The very book you now hold in your anxious, pug-loving hands? If Mike Norton had his way, it would have never existed. Not in a "You don't deserve my greatness!!" way, but more in a, "I never want to go through that again!!" way. See, these three stories were all created during 24-Hour Comics Day (http://24hourcomicsday.com/) wherein dedicated participants have 24-straight-hours to write and draw their own 24-page comic. Mike participated for the very first time in 2009, and "The Curse" was born. And like an actual birth, this book was ripped from inside of him, flailing and bloody as it was brought screaming into this world. Mike hated almost every second of it. But, and this is the important part, forcing yourself to be awake and creating for that long has lasting effects on the person doing it. Things… happen… And Mike? Man, he came out the other side angry, violent, disoriented, and in possession of one of the most important books he's created yet. And then he did it again. Twice more. For a total of three 24-Hour Comics Days, three years in a row.

I could spend this introduction telling the tales of Mike's bathrobe and pajama pants; the way he did more work sprawled on a couch while everyone around him worked furiously confined to tables; how the very second he finished the first volume his entire demeanor changed as if the heavens themselves shone down on him. Sure, he yelled. A lot. Yes, there MAY have been tears. But ultimately? Mike Norton produced a book that redefined his style. A comic that showed he's as good of a writer as he is an artist. And we learn that Mike is no stranger to profanity.

While it may be true Mike did NOT have fun making these comics, those of us around him did; we were there to witness each panel as it came to life. We were there to laugh at the absurdity that burst forth from Mike's sleep-deprived mind. We watched with wonder as he produced all of this just a with portable Mac and a stylus, and his crazy, crazy brain. And we loved it. And hopefully by now Mike loves it, too. Thank you, Mike Norton, for giving the world "The Curse."

Patrick Brower
Co-owner, Challengers Comics + Conversation

THE CURSE

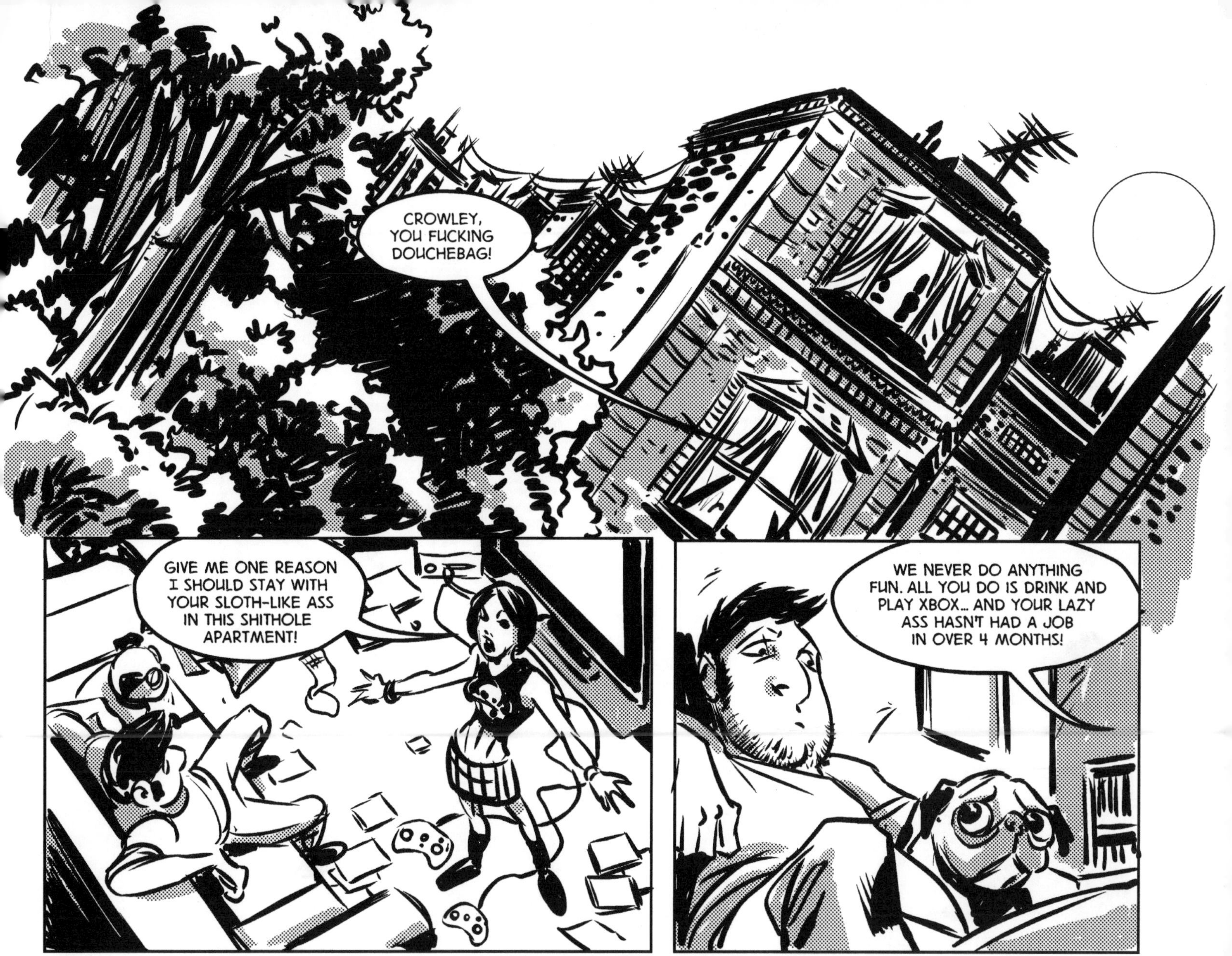
CROWLEY, YOU FUCKING DOUCHEBAG!
GIVE ME ONE REASON I SHOULD STAY WITH YOUR SLOTH-LIKE ASS IN THIS SHITHOLE APARTMENT!
WE NEVER DO ANYTHING FUN. ALL YOU DO IS DRINK AND PLAY XBOX... AND YOUR LAZY ASS HASN'T HAD A JOB IN OVER 4 MONTHS!

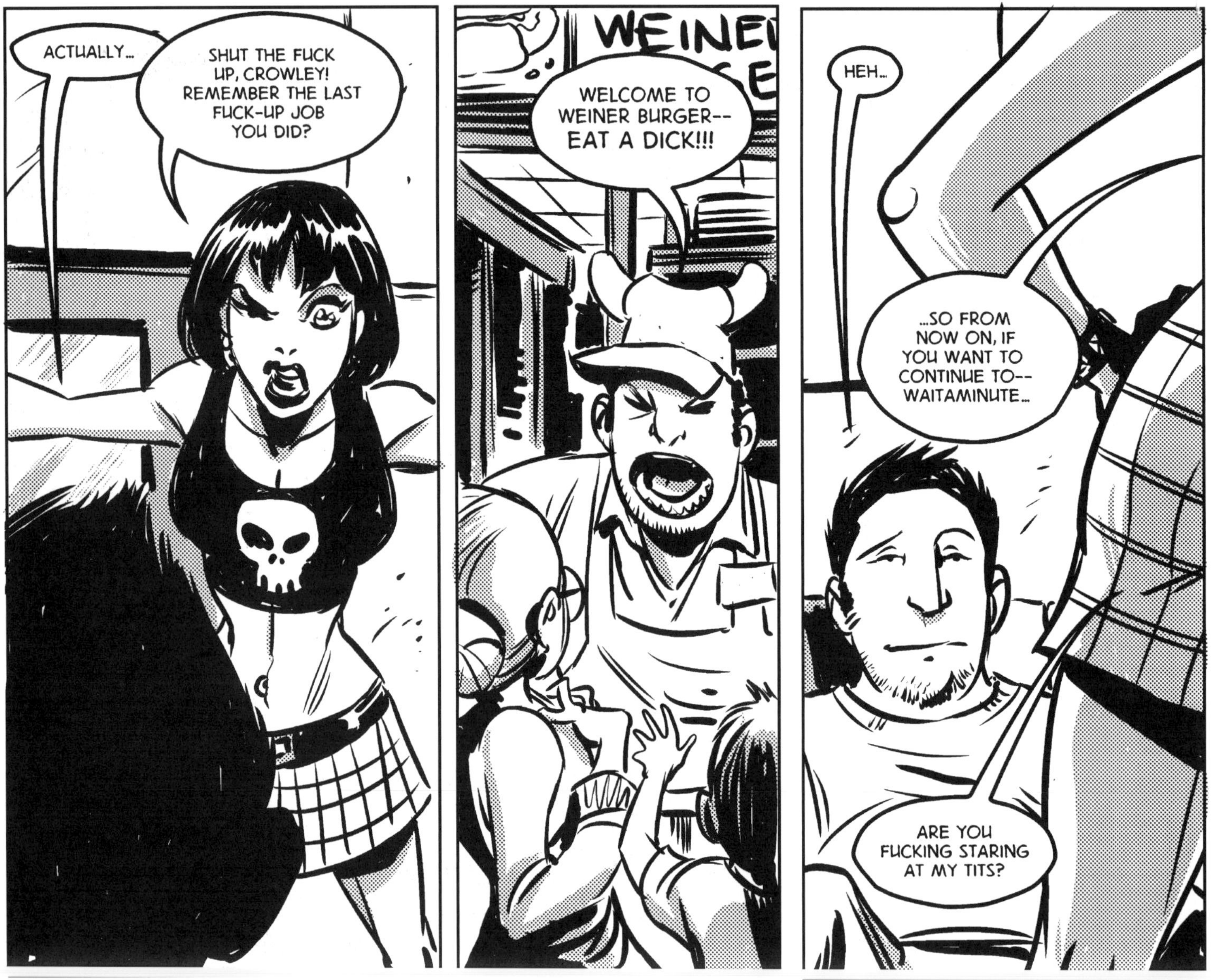
ACTUALLY...
SHUT THE FUCK UP, CROWLEY! REMEMBER THE LAST FUCK-UP JOB YOU DID?
WEINE
WELCOME TO WEINER BURGER-- EAT A DICK!!!
HEH...
...SO FROM NOW ON, IF YOU WANT TO CONTINUE TO-- WAITAMINUTE...
ARE YOU FUCKING STARING AT MY TITS?

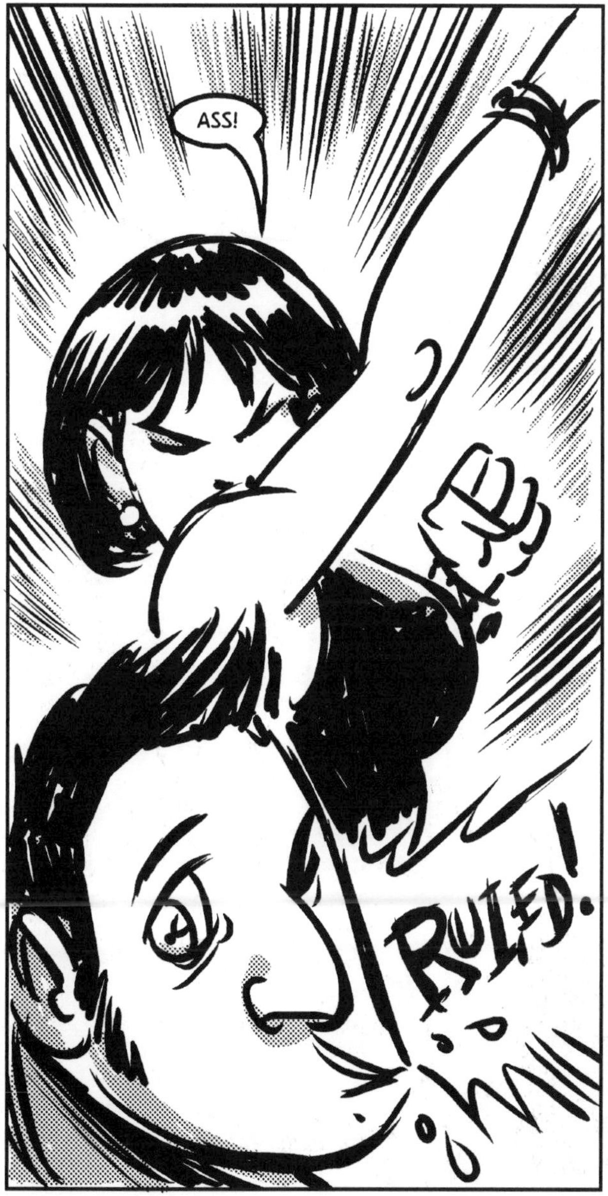
ASS!
RULED!

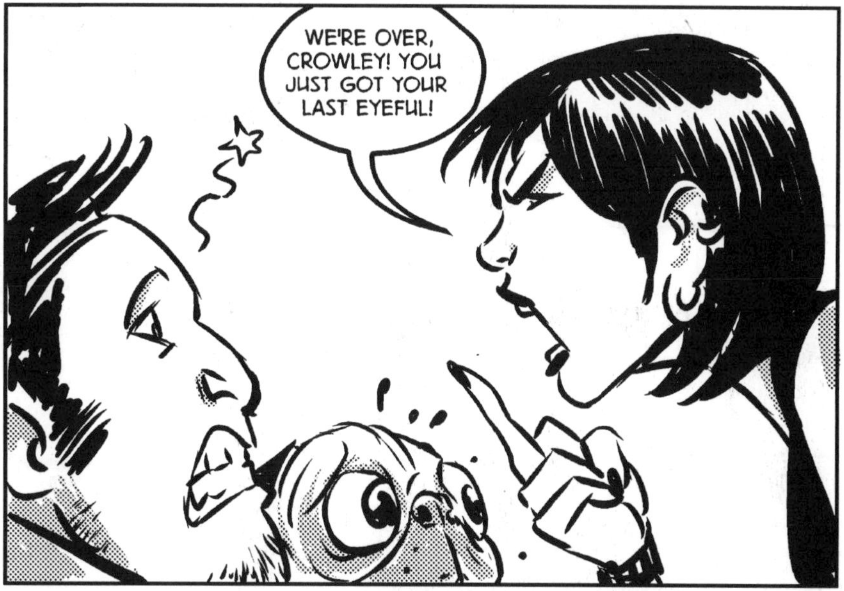
WE'RE OVER, CROWLEY! YOU JUST GOT YOUR LAST EYEFUL!

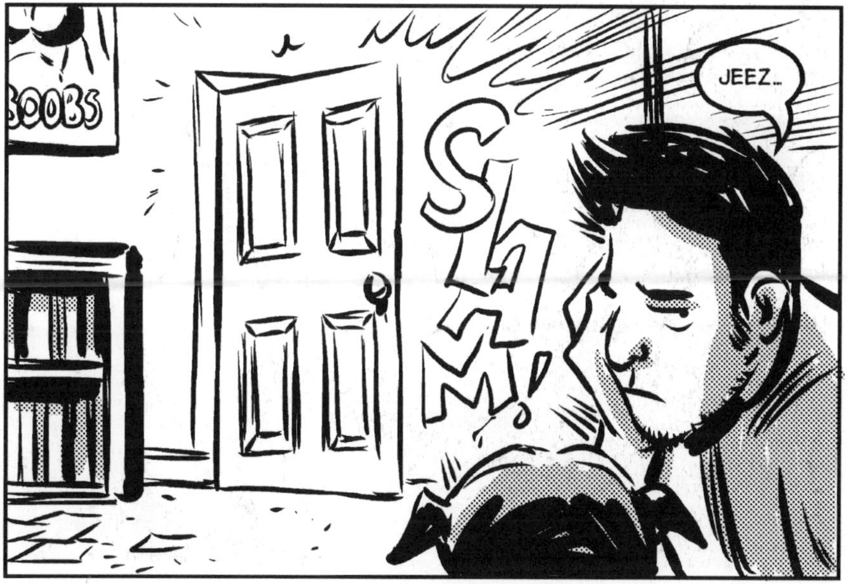
BOOBS
SLAM!
JEEZ...

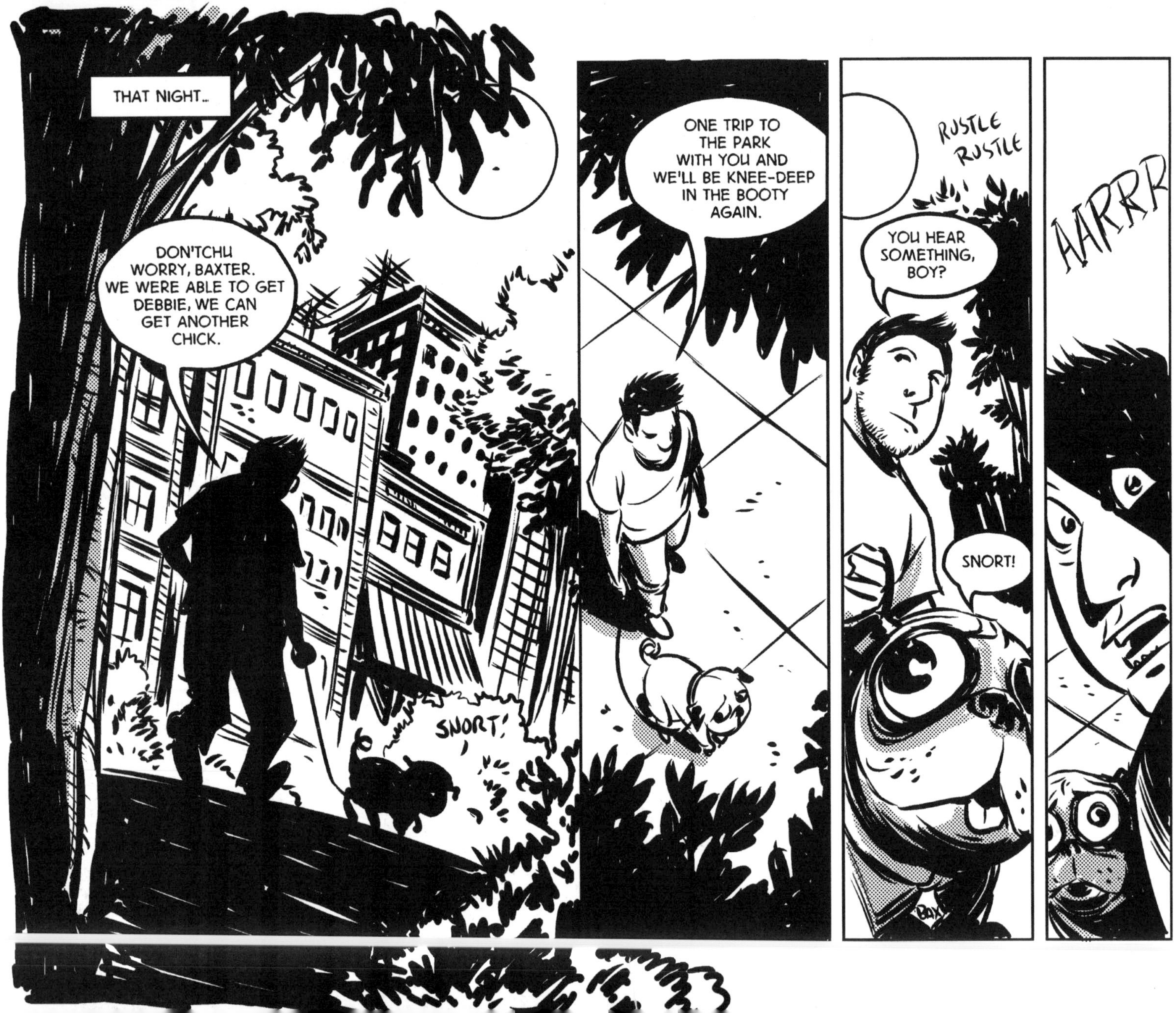
THAT NIGHT...
DON'TCHU WORRY, BAXTER. WE WERE ABLE TO GET DEBBIE, WE CAN GET ANOTHER CHICK.
SNORT!
ONE TRIP TO THE PARK WITH YOU AND WE'LL BE KNEE-DEEP IN THE BOOTY AGAIN.
RUSTLE RUSTLE
YOU HEAR SOMETHING, BOY?
SNORT!
AARRR

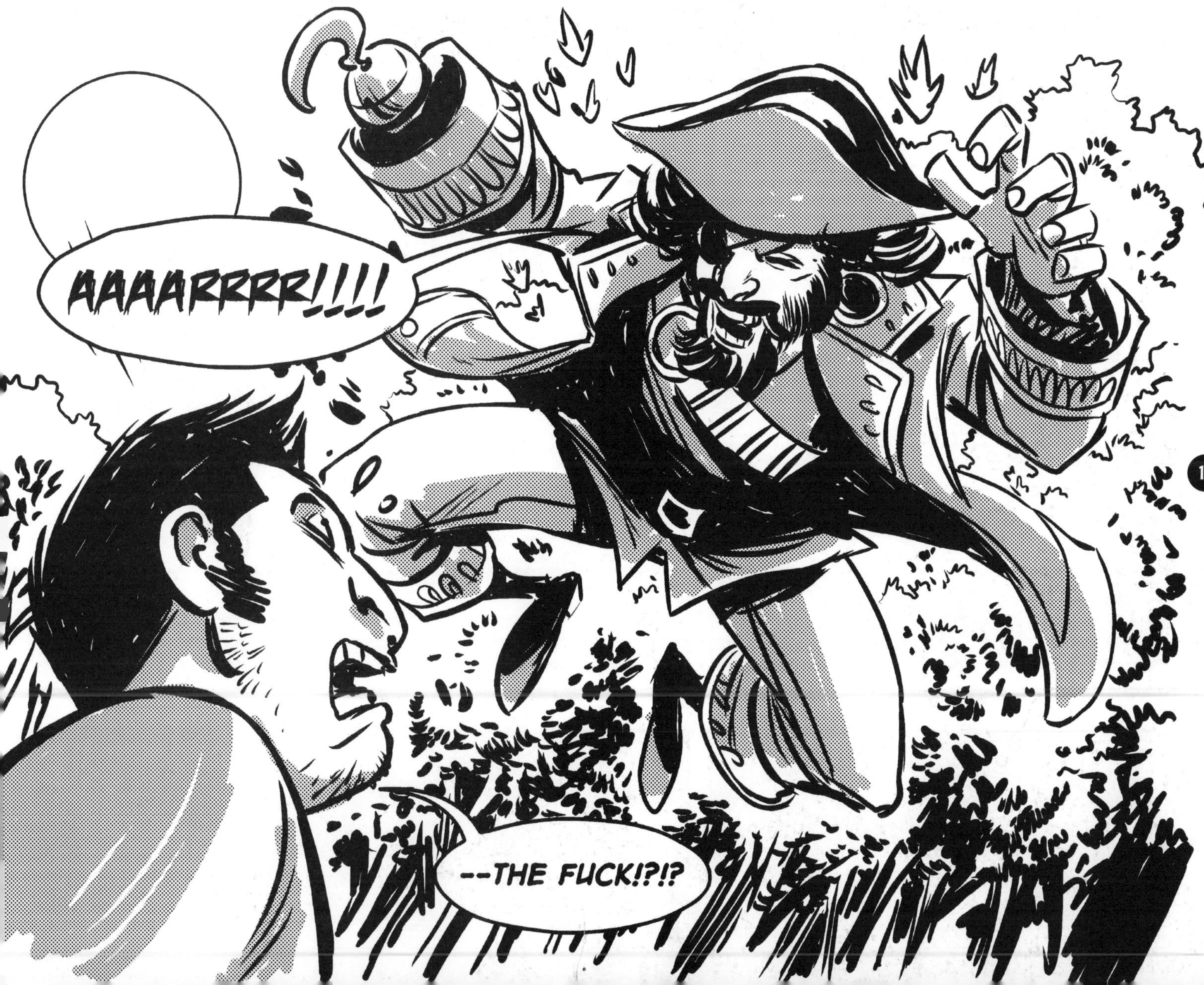
AAAARRRR!!!!
--THE FUCK!?!?

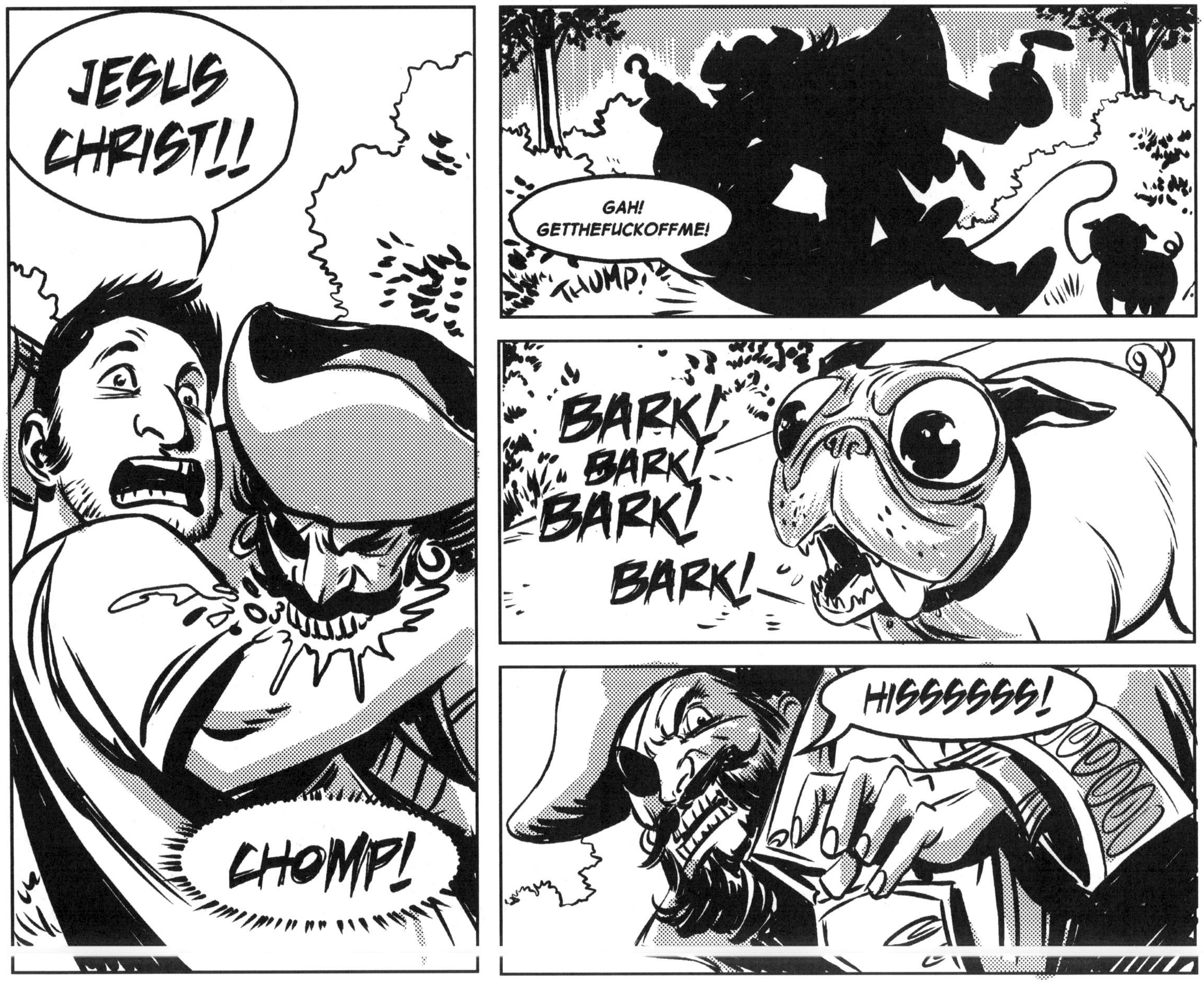
JESUS CHRIST!!
CHOMP!
GAH! GETTHEFUCKOFFME!
THUMP!
BARK!
BARK!
BARK!
BARK!
HISSSSSS!

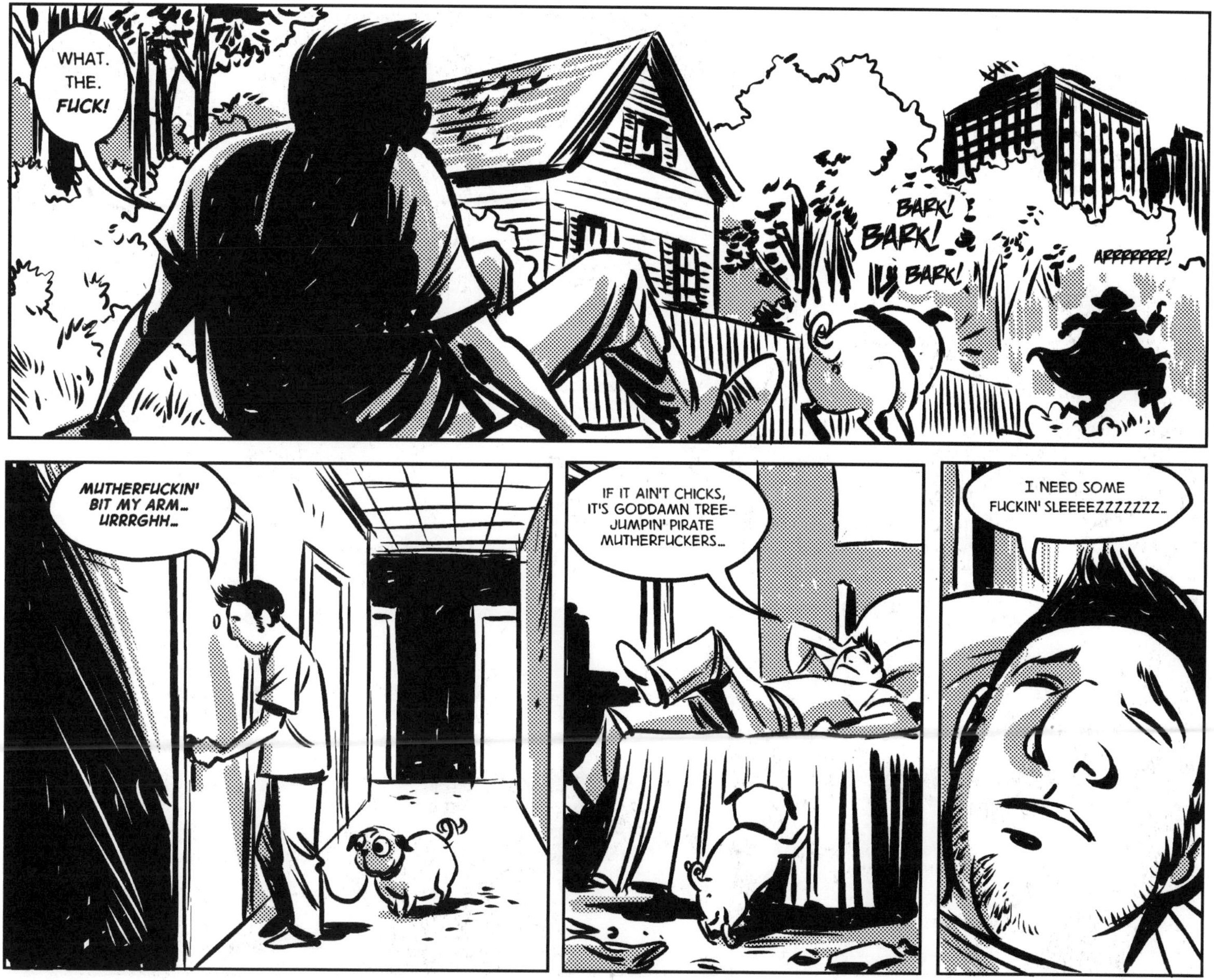

WHAT. THE. *FUCK!*
BARK!
BARK!
BARK!
ARRRRRRR!
MUTHERFUCKIN' BIT MY ARM... URRRGHH...
IF IT AIN'T CHICKS, IT'S GODDAMN TREE-JUMPIN' PIRATE MUTHERFUCKERS...
I NEED SOME FUCKIN' SLEEEEZZZZZZZ...

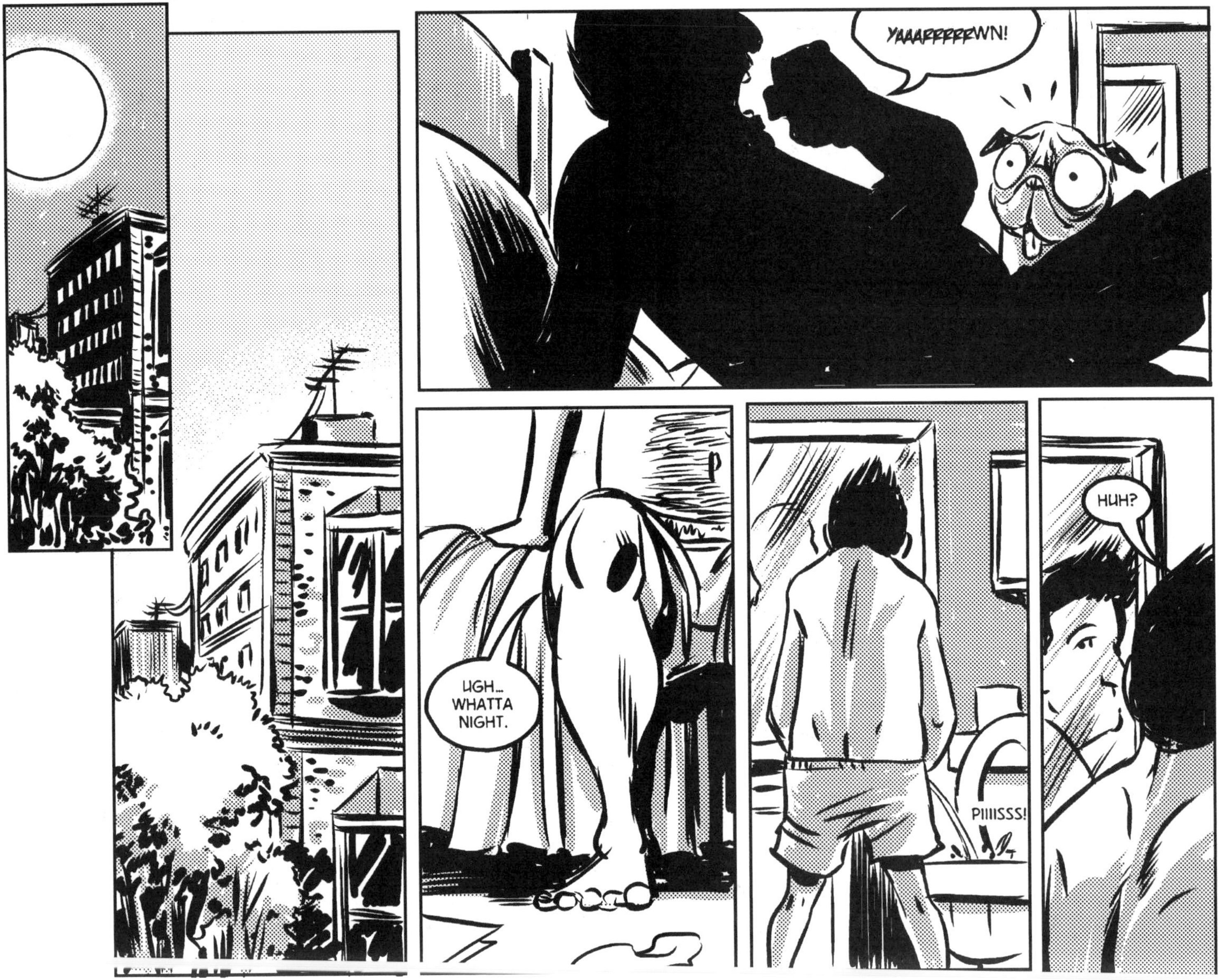
YAAARRRRRWN!
UGH... WHATTA NIGHT.
PIIIISSS!
HUH?

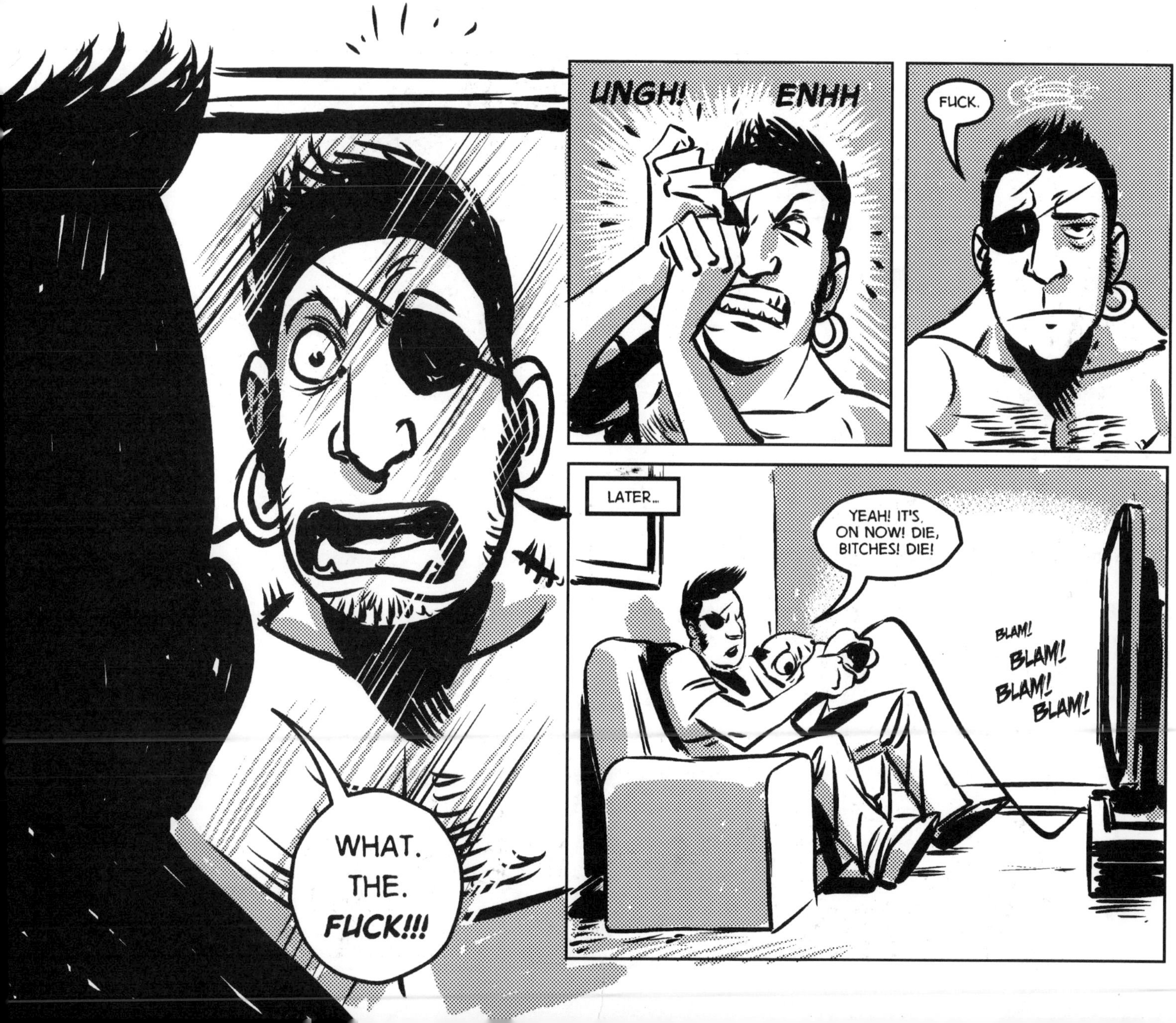
WHAT. THE. FUCK!!!
UNGH! ENHH
FUCK.
LATER...
YEAH! IT'S, ON NOW! DIE, BITCHES! DIE!
BLAM! BLAM! BLAM! BLAM!

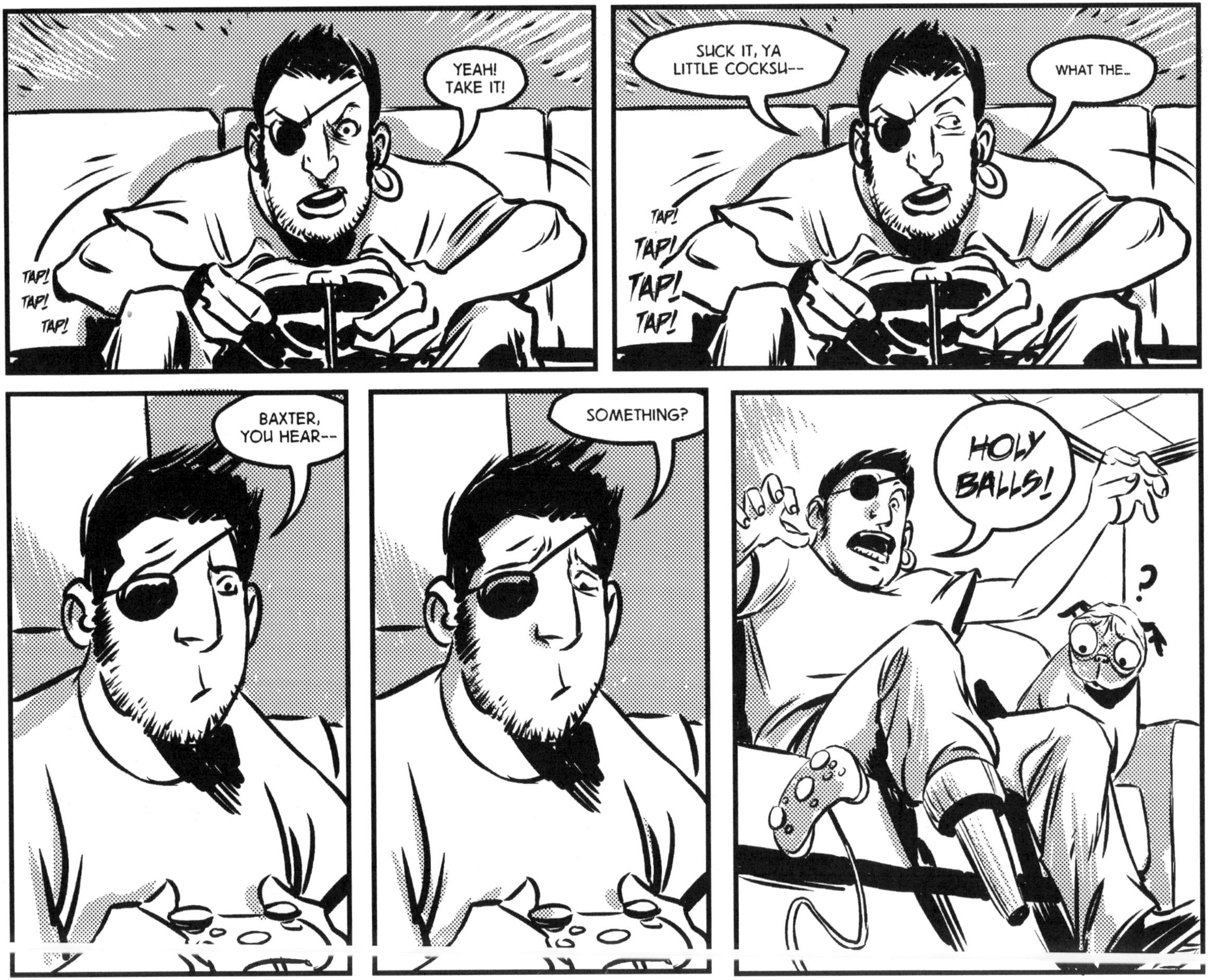
YEAH! TAKE IT!
TAP! TAP! TAP!
SUCK IT, YA LITTLE COCKSU--
WHAT THE..
TAP! TAP! TAP! TAP!
BAXTER, YOU HEAR--
SOMETHING?
HOLY BALLS!
?

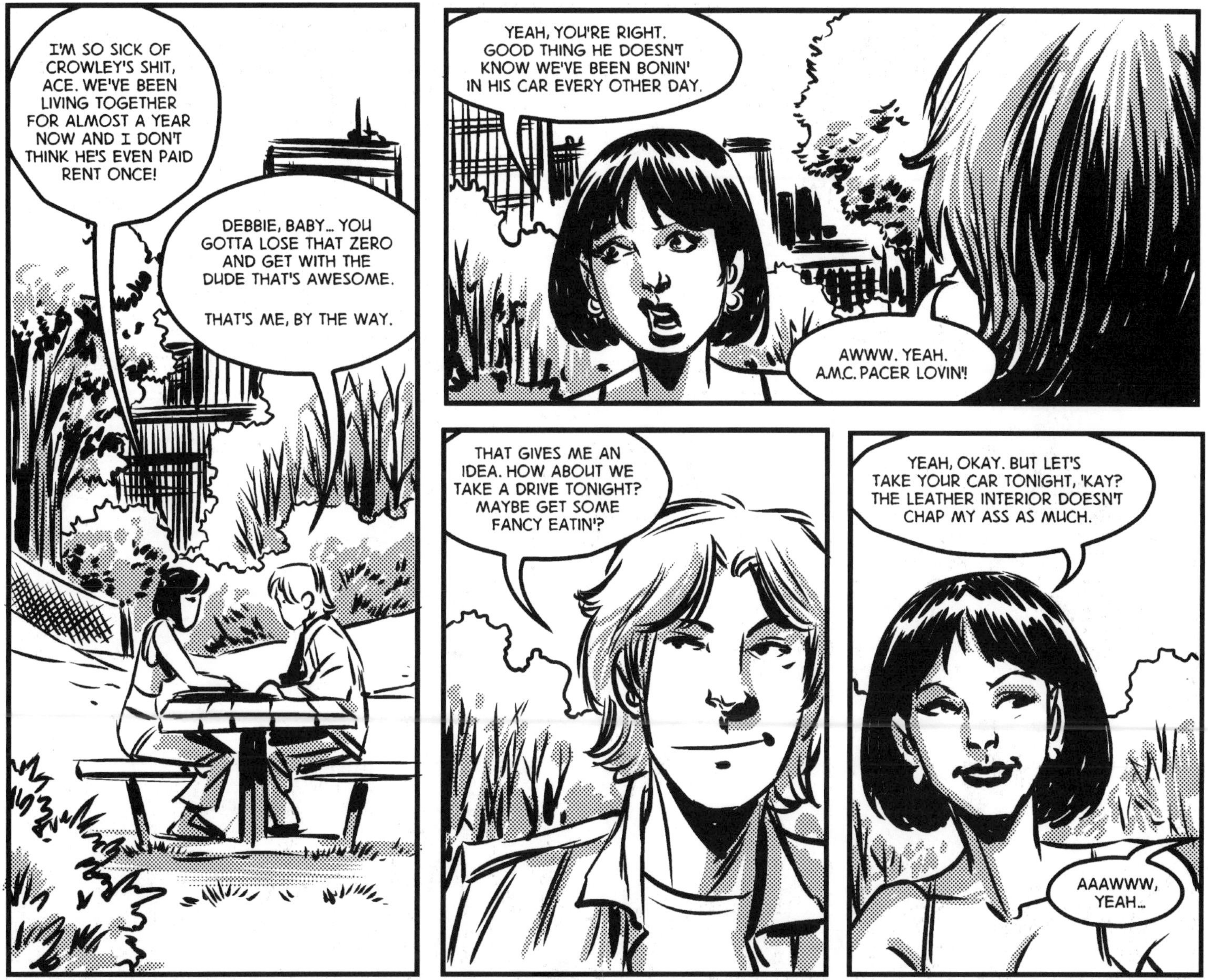

I'M SO SICK OF CROWLEY'S SHIT, ACE. WE'VE BEEN LIVING TOGETHER FOR ALMOST A YEAR NOW AND I DON'T THINK HE'S EVEN PAID RENT ONCE!
DEBBIE, BABY... YOU GOTTA LOSE THAT ZERO AND GET WITH THE DUDE THAT'S AWESOME.
THAT'S ME, BY THE WAY.
YEAH, YOU'RE RIGHT. GOOD THING HE DOESN'T KNOW WE'VE BEEN BONIN' IN HIS CAR EVERY OTHER DAY.
AWWW. YEAH. A.M.C. PACER LOVIN'!
THAT GIVES ME AN IDEA. HOW ABOUT WE TAKE A DRIVE TONIGHT? MAYBE GET SOME FANCY EATIN'?
YEAH, OKAY. BUT LET'S TAKE YOUR CAR TONIGHT, 'KAY? THE LEATHER INTERIOR DOESN'T CHAP MY ASS AS MUCH.
AAAWWW, YEAH...

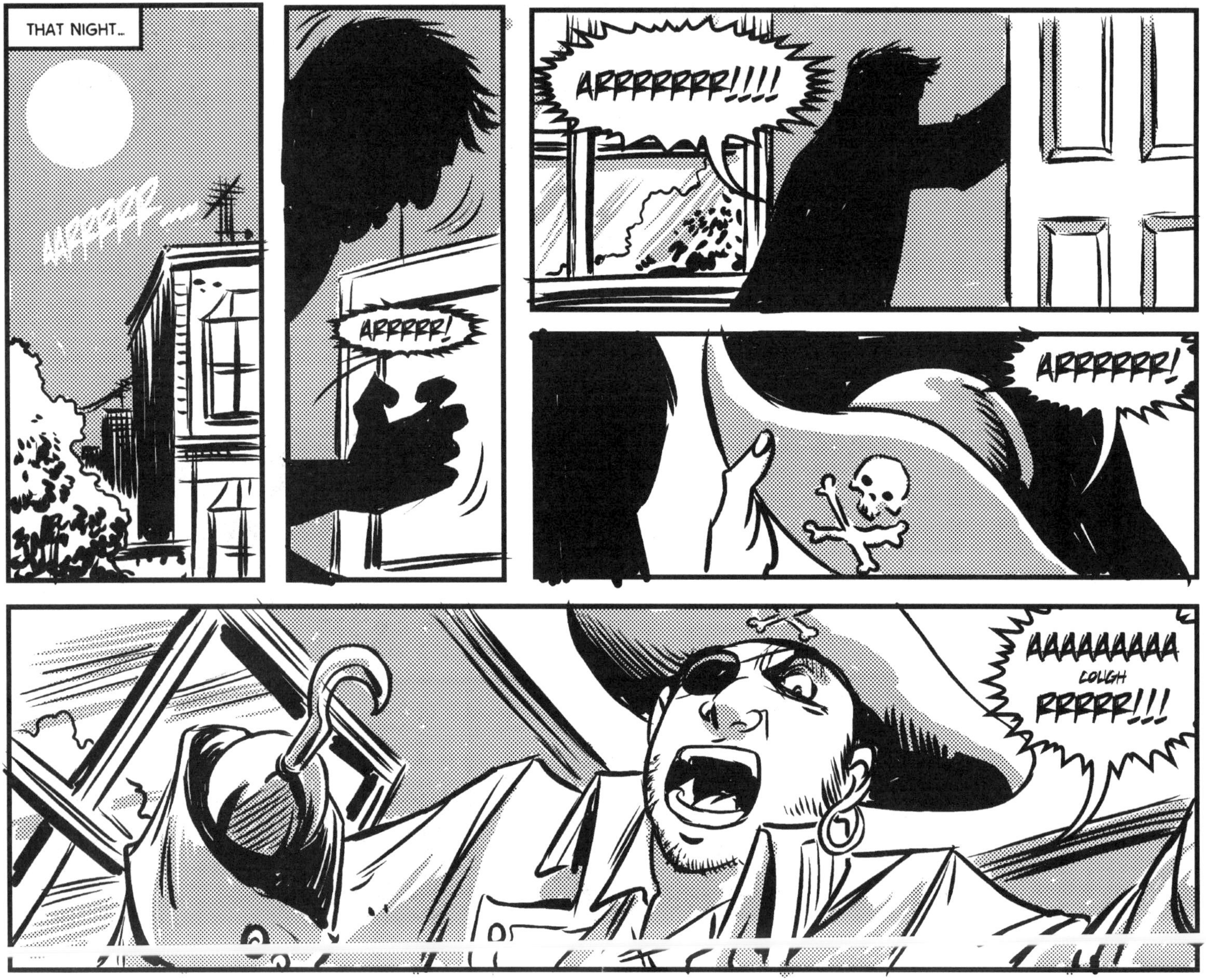
THAT NIGHT...
AARRRRR...
ARRRRR!
ARRRRRRRR!!!!
ARRRRRR!
AAAAAAAAA
COUGH
RRRRR!!!

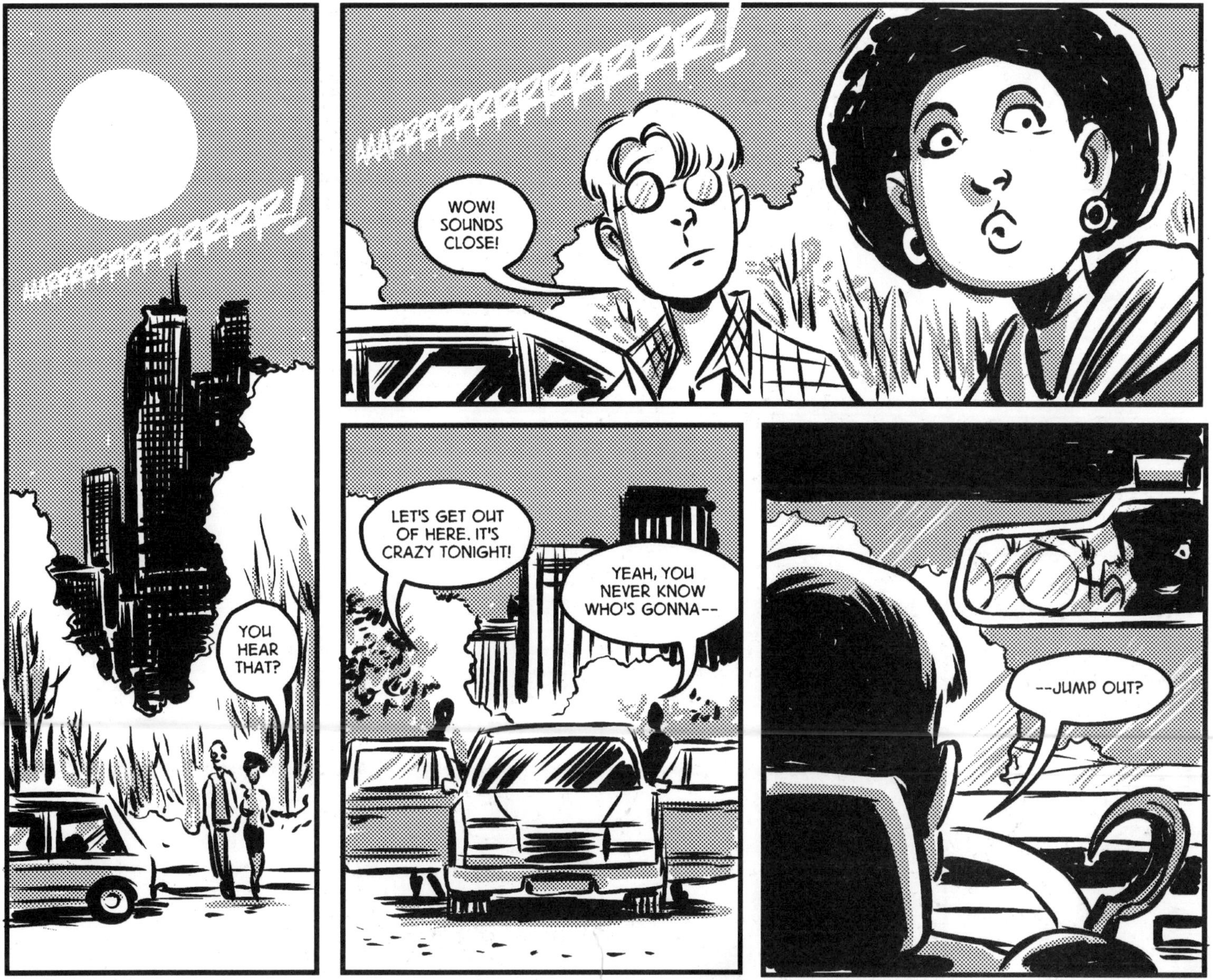
AAARRRRRRRRRRRRRR!
YOU HEAR THAT?
AAARRRRRRRRRRRRRRRRR!
WOW! SOUNDS CLOSE!
LET'S GET OUT OF HERE. IT'S CRAZY TONIGHT!
YEAH, YOU NEVER KNOW WHO'S GONNA--
--JUMP OUT?

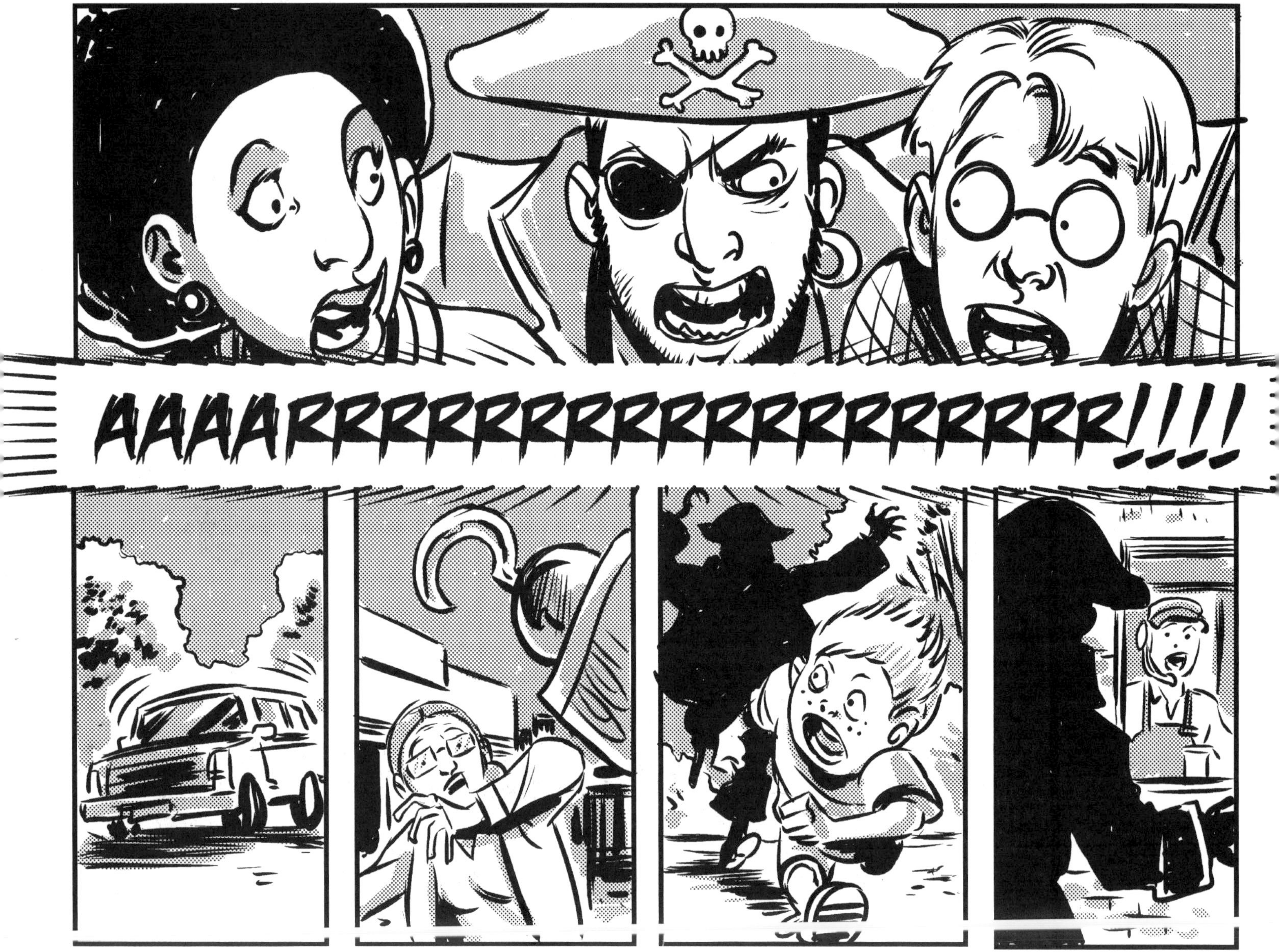
AAAARRRRRRRRRRRRRRRRRRRRR!!!!

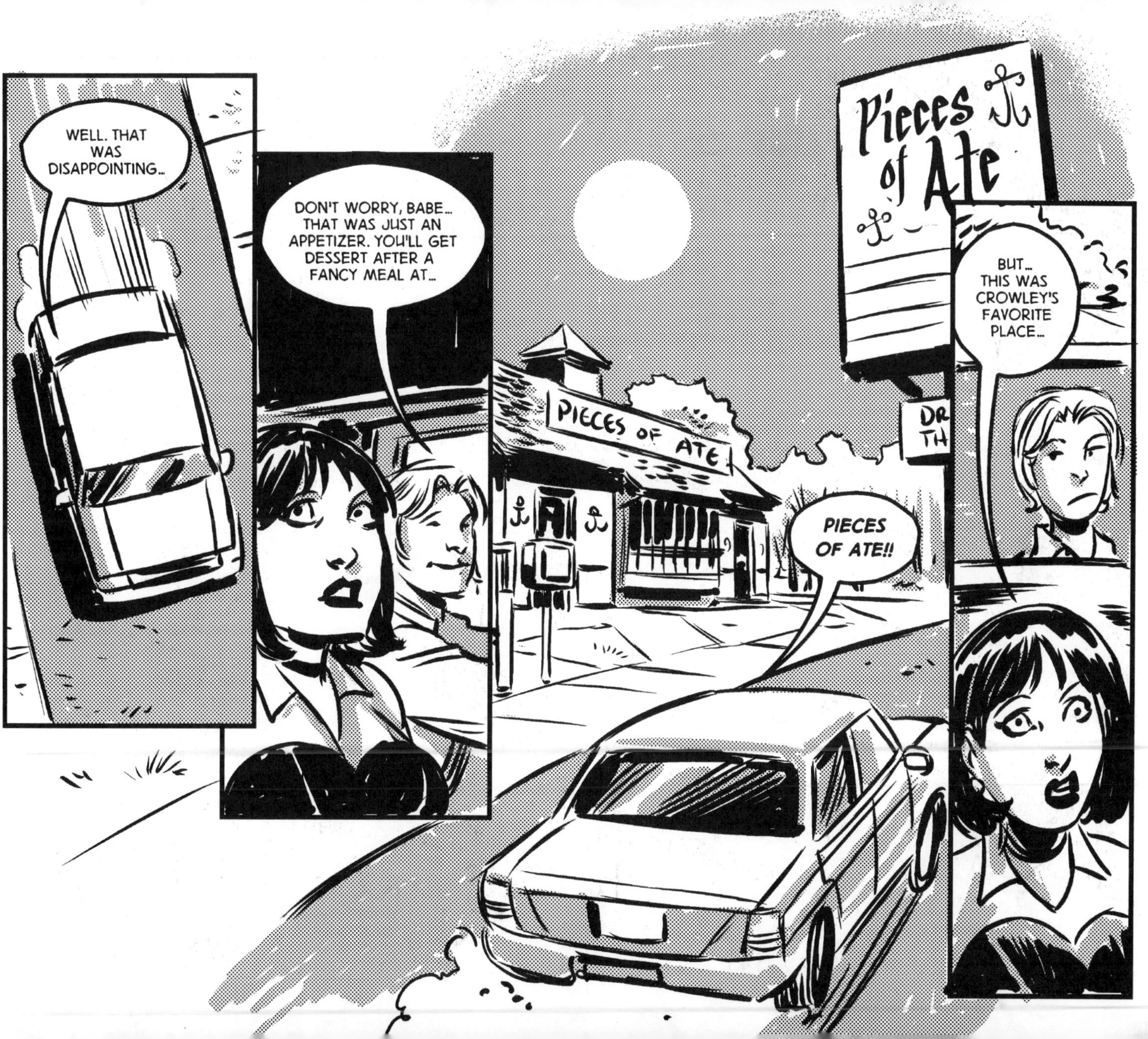
WELL. THAT WAS DISAPPOINTING...
DON'T WORRY, BABE... THAT WAS JUST AN APPETIZER. YOU'LL GET DESSERT AFTER A FANCY MEAL AT...
Pieces of Ate
PIECES OF ATE
PIECES OF ATE!!
BUT... THIS WAS CROWLEY'S FAVORITE PLACE...

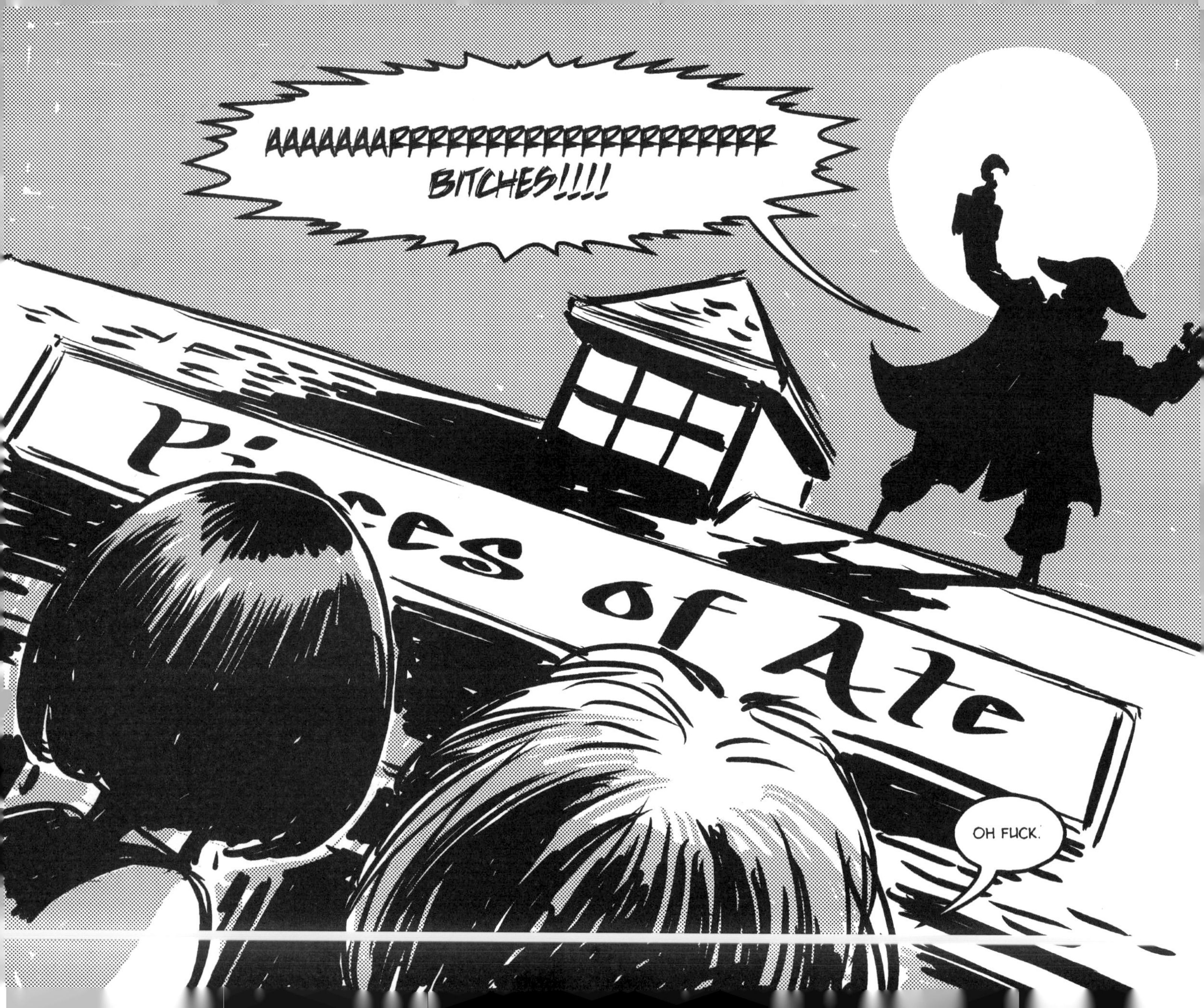
AAAAAAARRRRRRRRRRRRRRRRRRRR
BITCHES!!!!!
OH FUCK.

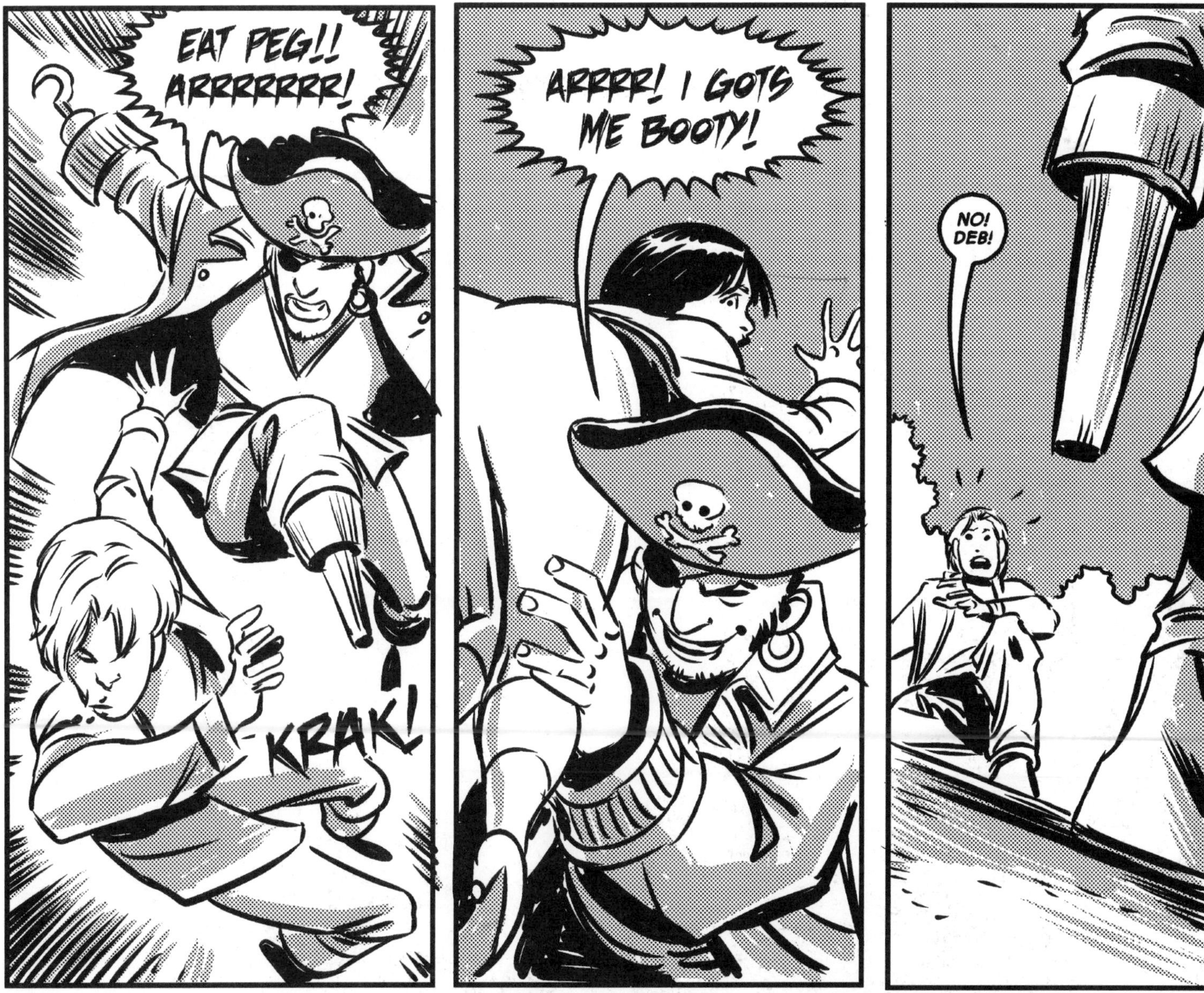
EAT PEG!! ARRRRRRR!
KRAK!
ARRRR! I GOTS ME BOOTY!
NO! DEB!

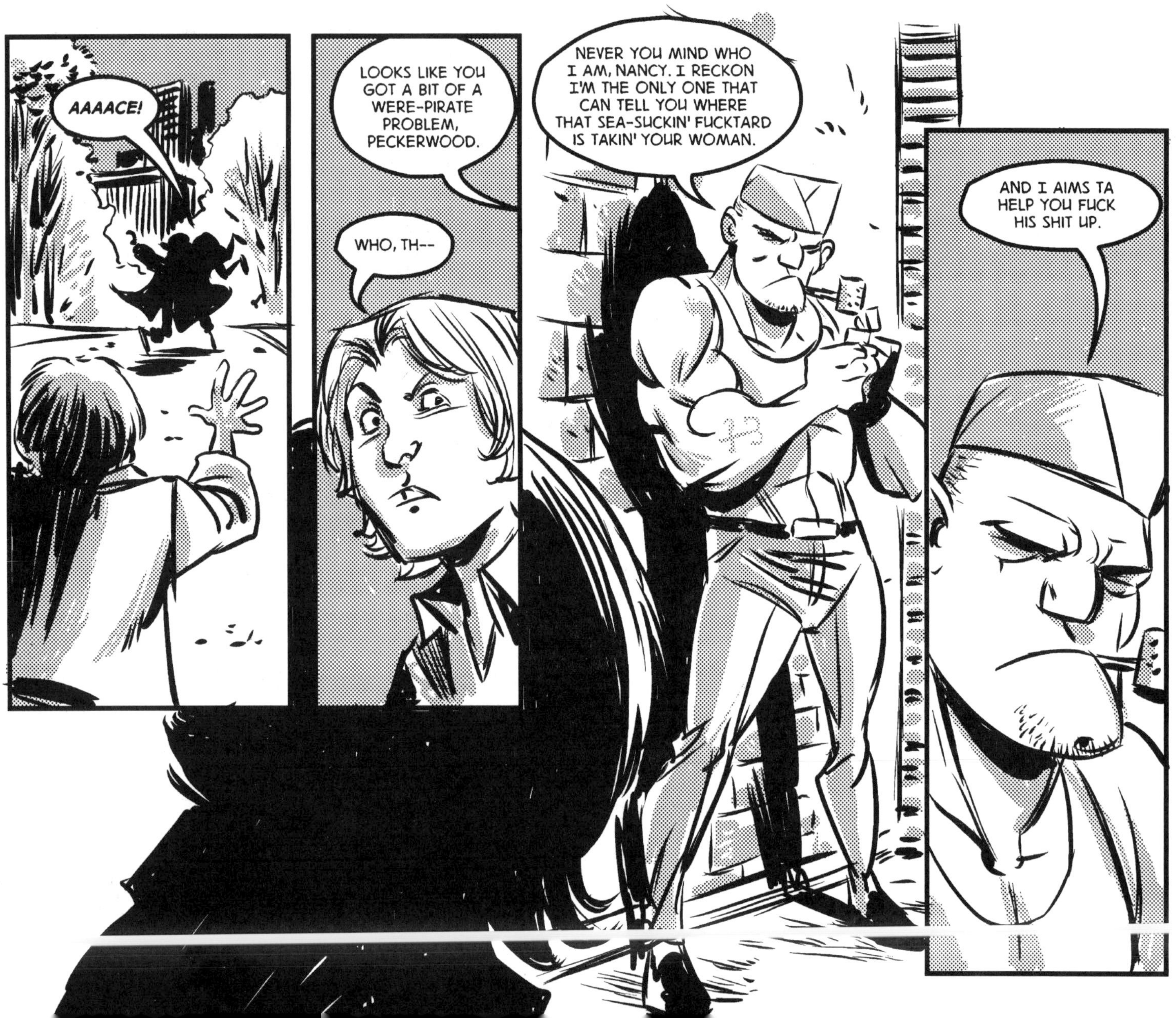
AAAACE!
LOOKS LIKE YOU GOT A BIT OF A WERE-PIRATE PROBLEM, PECKERWOOD.
WHO, TH--
NEVER YOU MIND WHO I AM, NANCY. I RECKON I'M THE ONLY ONE THAT CAN TELL YOU WHERE THAT SEA-SUCKIN' FUCKTARD IS TAKIN' YOUR WOMAN.
AND I AIMS TA HELP YOU FUCK HIS SHIT UP.

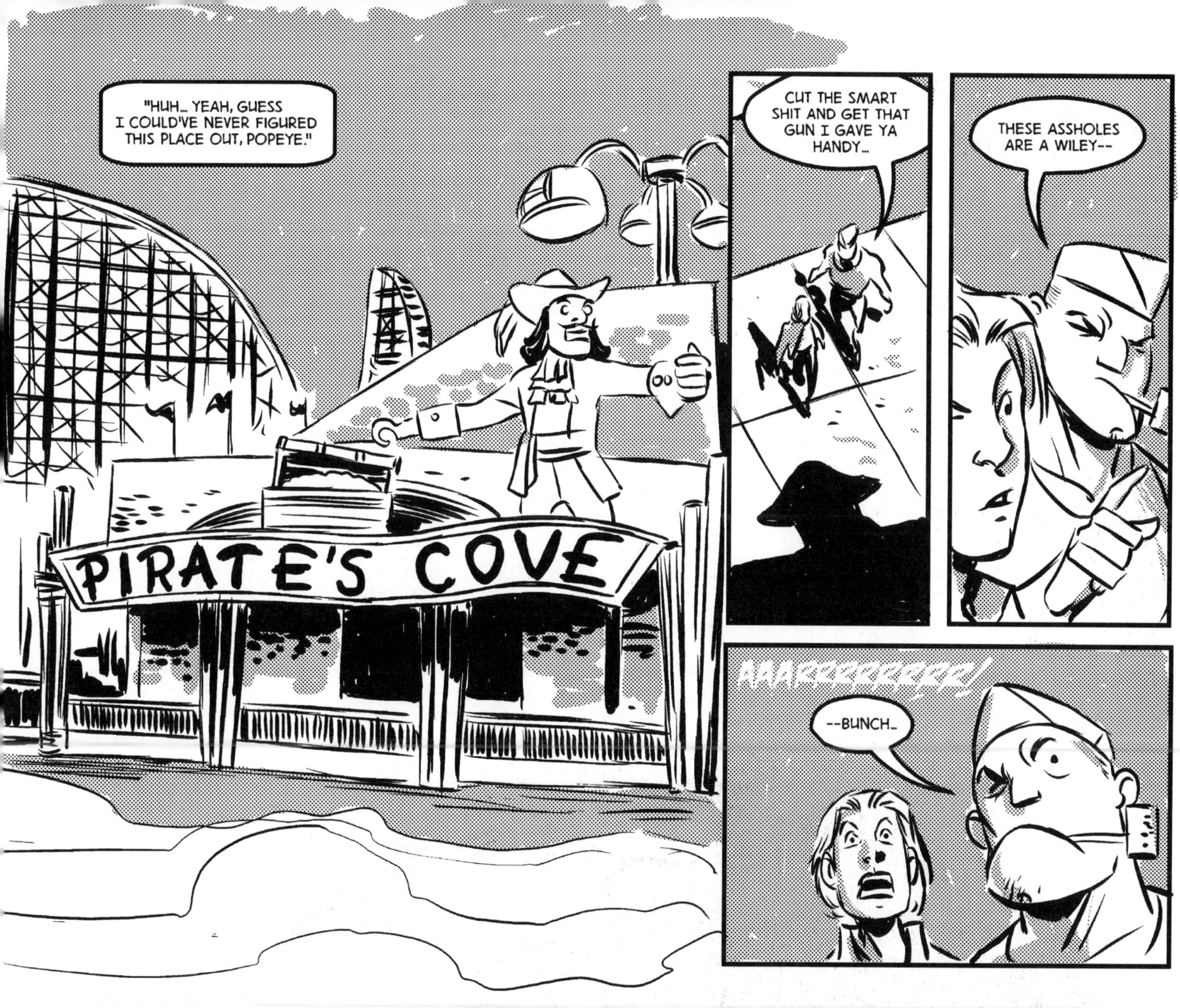
"HUH... YEAH, GUESS I COULD'VE NEVER FIGURED THIS PLACE OUT, POPEYE."
PIRATE'S COVE
CUT THE SMART SHIT AND GET THAT GUN I GAVE YA HANDY...
THESE ASSHOLES ARE A WILEY--
AAARRRRRRRRR!
--BUNCH...

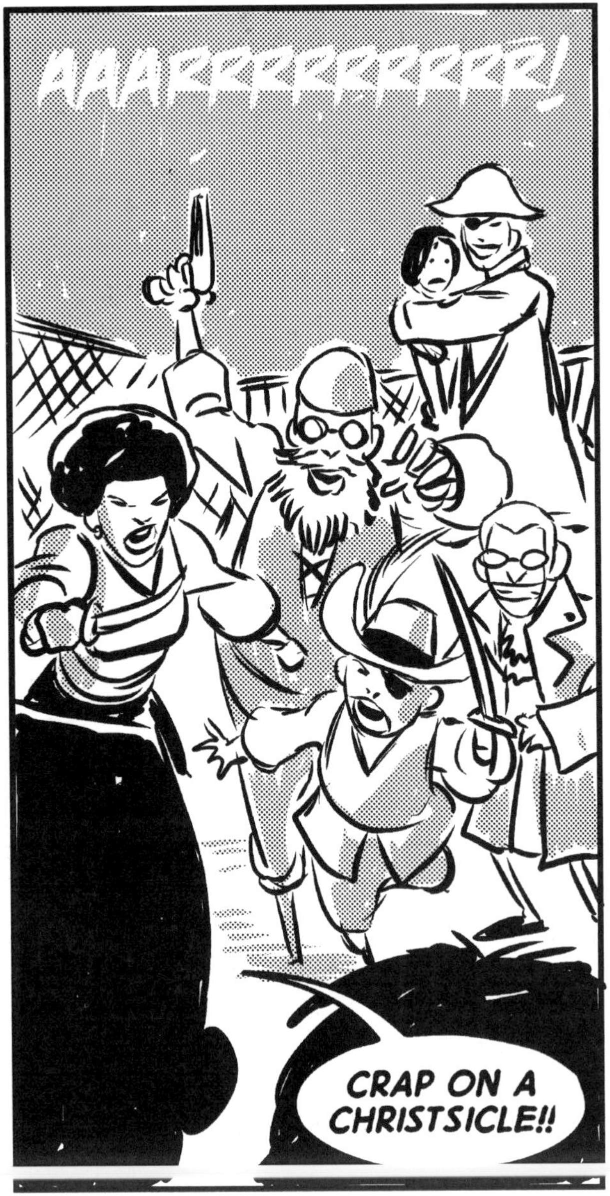

AAARRRRRRRRRRR!
CRAP ON A CHRISTSICLE!!

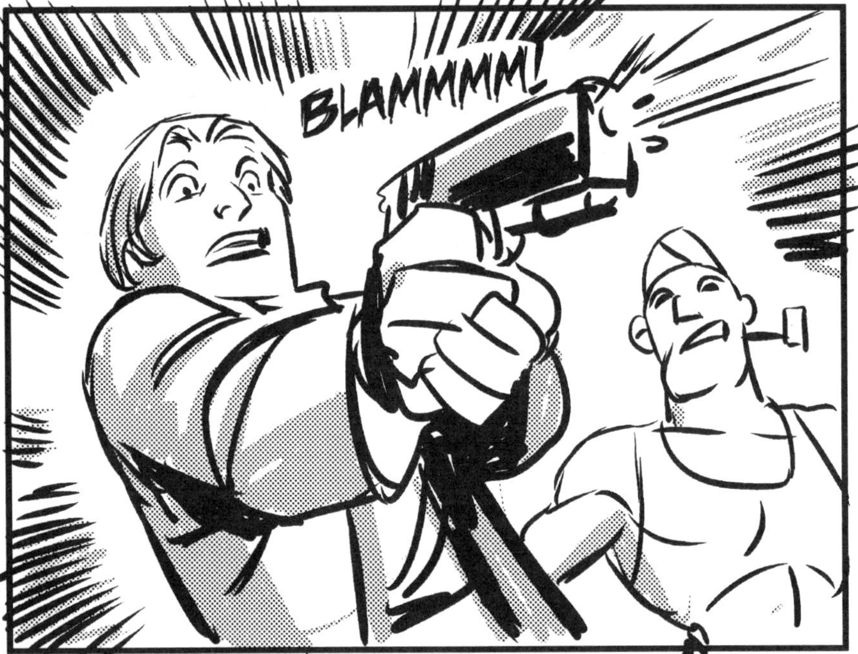

BLAMMMM!

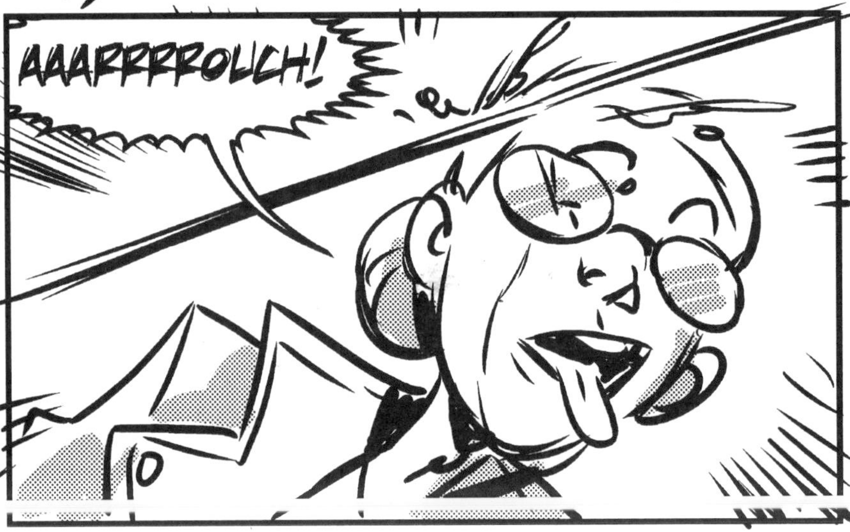

AAARRRROUCH!

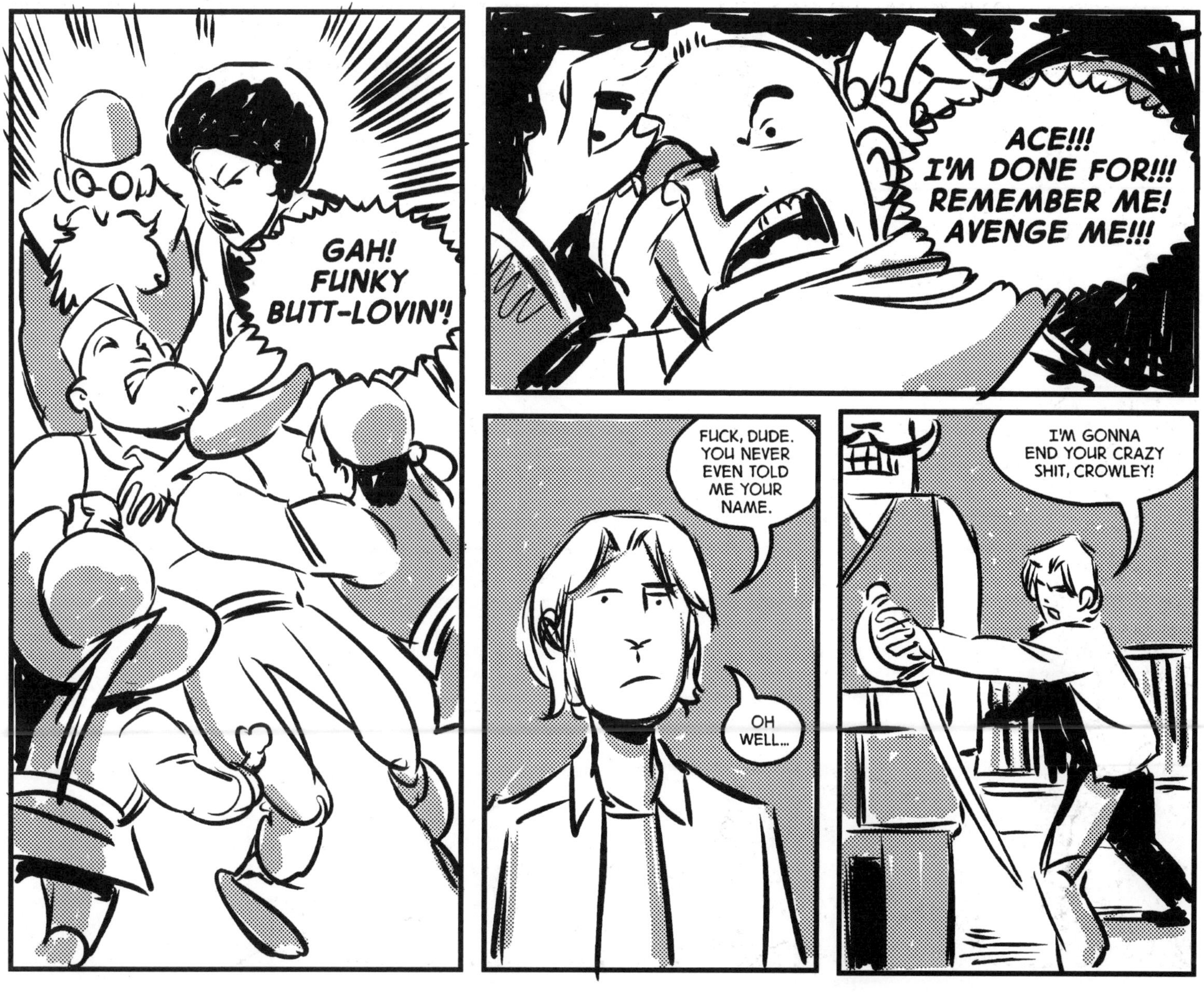
GAH! FUNKY BUTT-LOVIN'!
ACE!!! I'M DONE FOR!!! REMEMBER ME! AVENGE ME!!!
FUCK, DUDE. YOU NEVER EVEN TOLD ME YOUR NAME.
OH WELL...
I'M GONNA END YOUR CRAZY SHIT, CROWLEY!

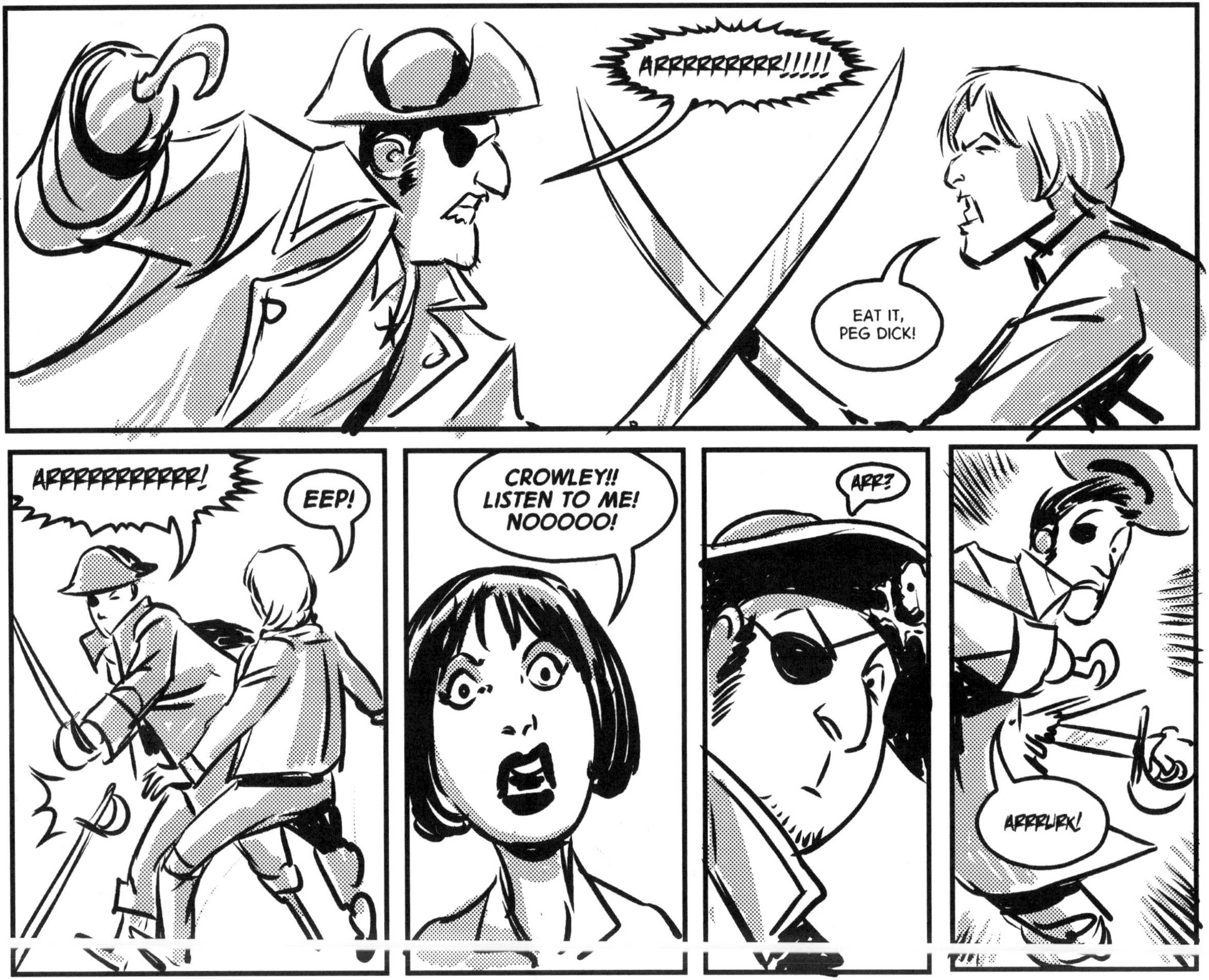
ARRRRRRRRR!!!!!
EAT IT, PEG DICK!
ARRRRRRRRRRR!
EEP!
CROWLEY!! LISTEN TO ME! NOOOOO!
ARR?
ARRRLURK!

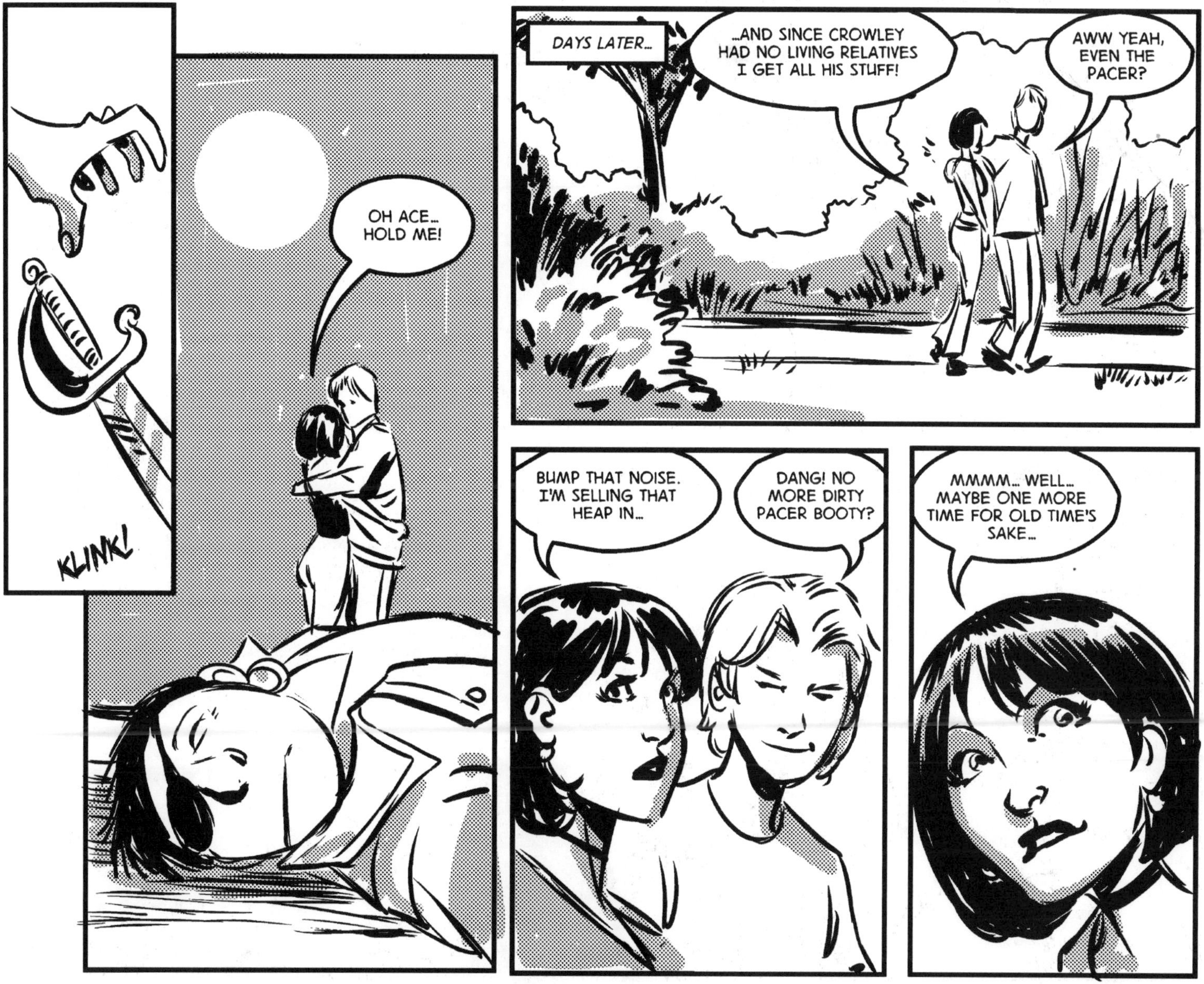
KLINK!
OH ACE... HOLD ME!
DAYS LATER...
...AND SINCE CROWLEY HAD NO LIVING RELATIVES I GET ALL HIS STUFF!
AWW YEAH, EVEN THE PACER?
BUMP THAT NOISE. I'M SELLING THAT HEAP IN...
DANG! NO MORE DIRTY PACER BOOTY?
MMMM... WELL... MAYBE ONE MORE TIME FOR OLD TIME'S SAKE...

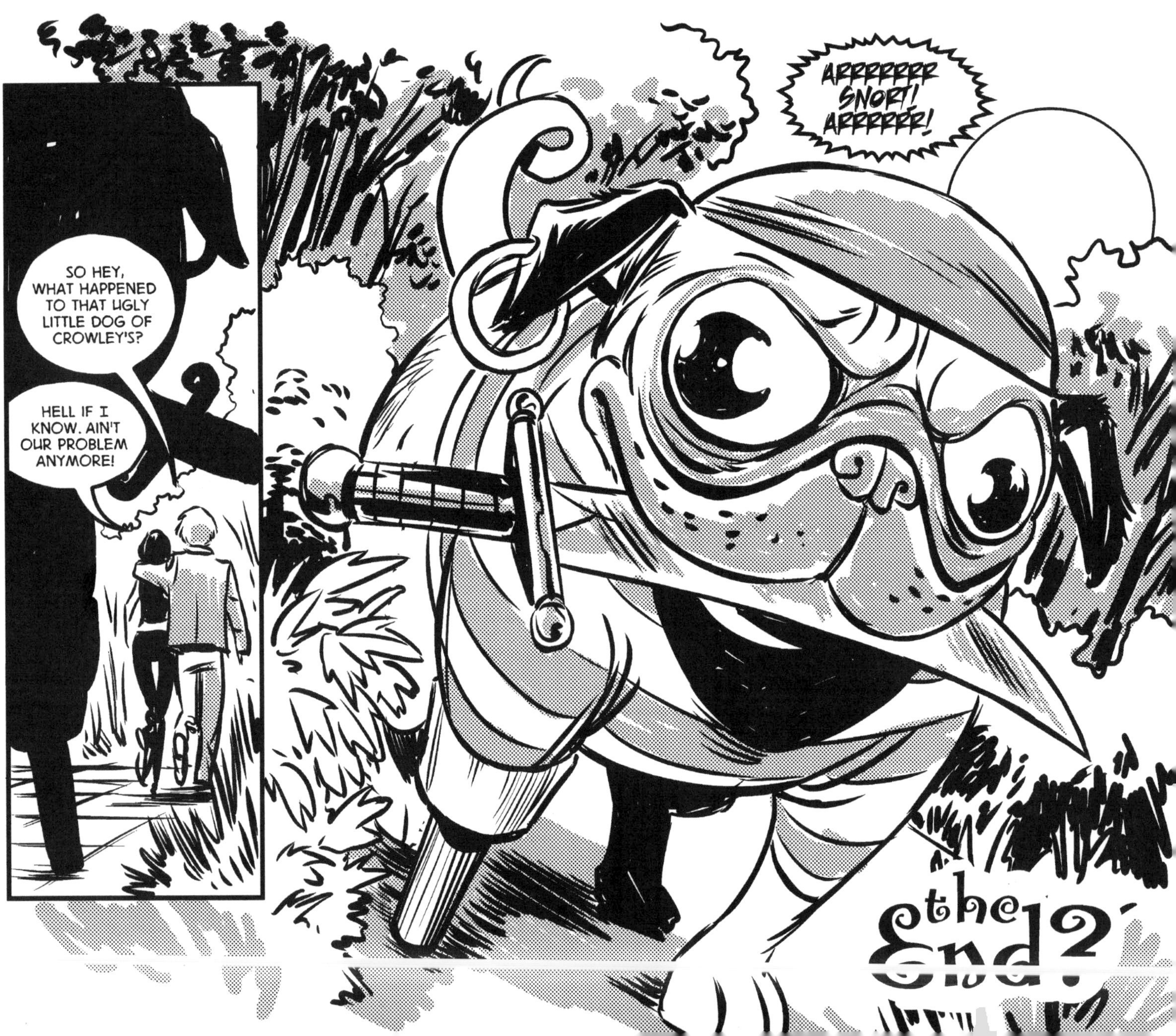
SO HEY, WHAT HAPPENED TO THAT UGLY LITTLE DOG OF CROWLEY'S?
HELL IF I KNOW. AIN'T OUR PROBLEM ANYMORE!
ARRRRRRR SNORT! ARRRRRR!
the End?

THE CURSE II:
THE CURSONING

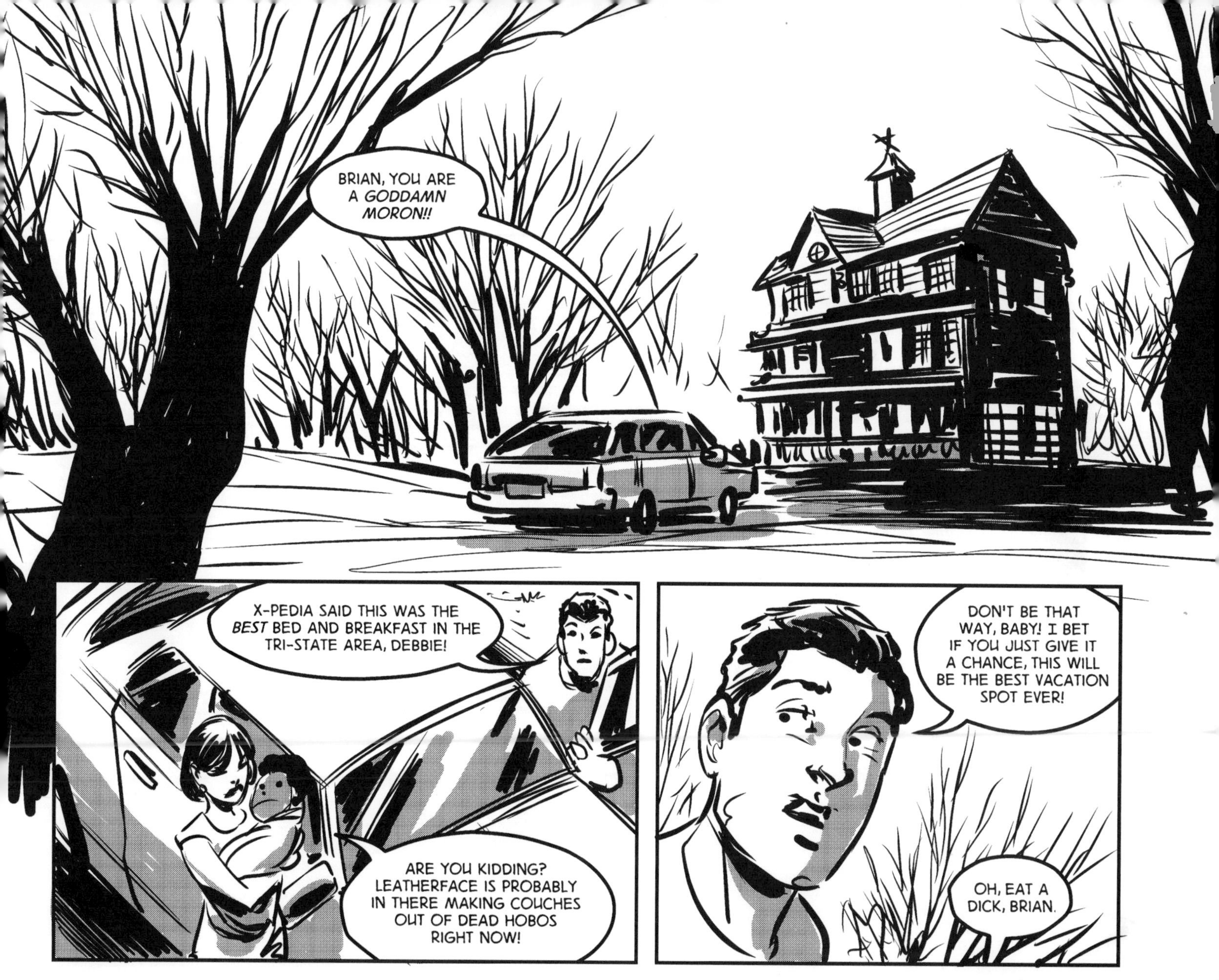
BRIAN, YOU ARE A *GODDAMN MORON!!*
X-PEDIA SAID THIS WAS THE *BEST* BED AND BREAKFAST IN THE TRI-STATE AREA, DEBBIE!
ARE YOU KIDDING? LEATHERFACE IS PROBABLY IN THERE MAKING COUCHES OUT OF DEAD HOBOS RIGHT NOW!
DON'T BE THAT WAY, BABY! I BET IF YOU JUST GIVE IT A CHANCE, THIS WILL BE THE BEST VACATION SPOT EVER!
OH, EAT A DICK, BRIAN.

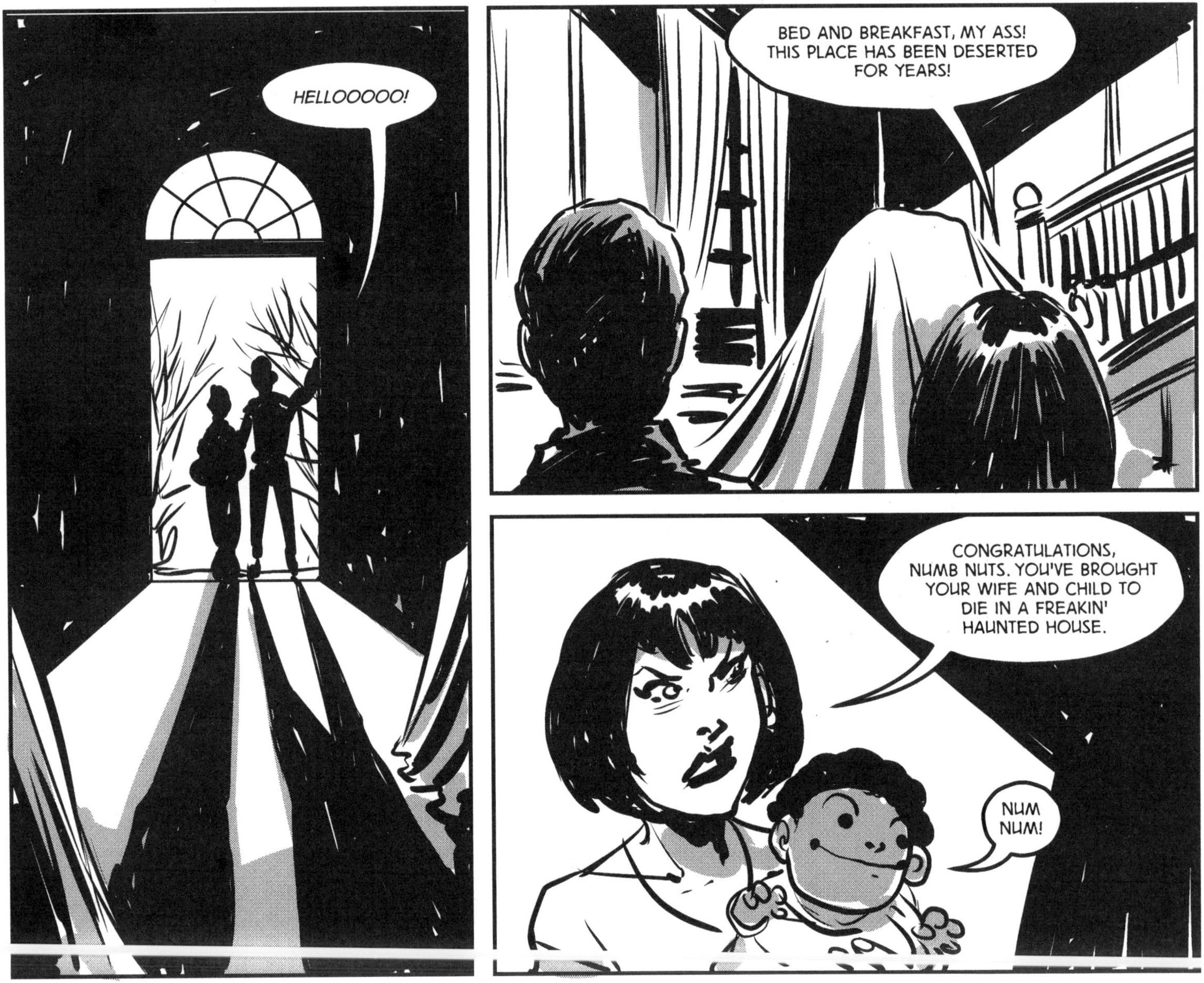
HELLOOOOO!
BED AND BREAKFAST, MY ASS! THIS PLACE HAS BEEN DESERTED FOR YEARS!
CONGRATULATIONS, NUMB NUTS. YOU'VE BROUGHT YOUR WIFE AND CHILD TO DIE IN A FREAKIN' HAUNTED HOUSE.
NUM NUM!

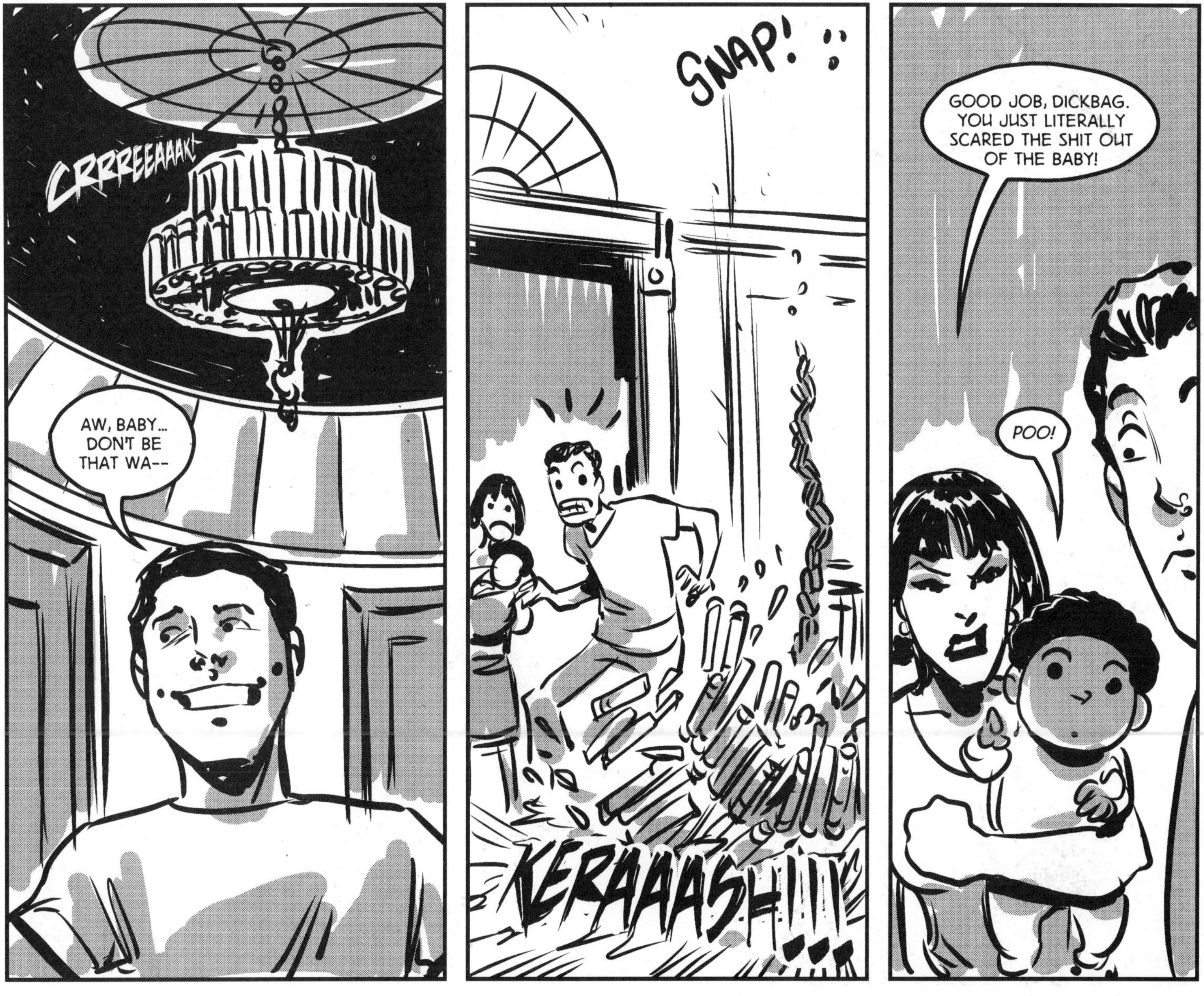
CRRREEAAAK!
AW, BABY... DON'T BE THAT WA--
SNAP!
KERAAASH!!!
GOOD JOB, DICKBAG. YOU JUST LITERALLY SCARED THE SHIT OUT OF THE BABY!
POO!

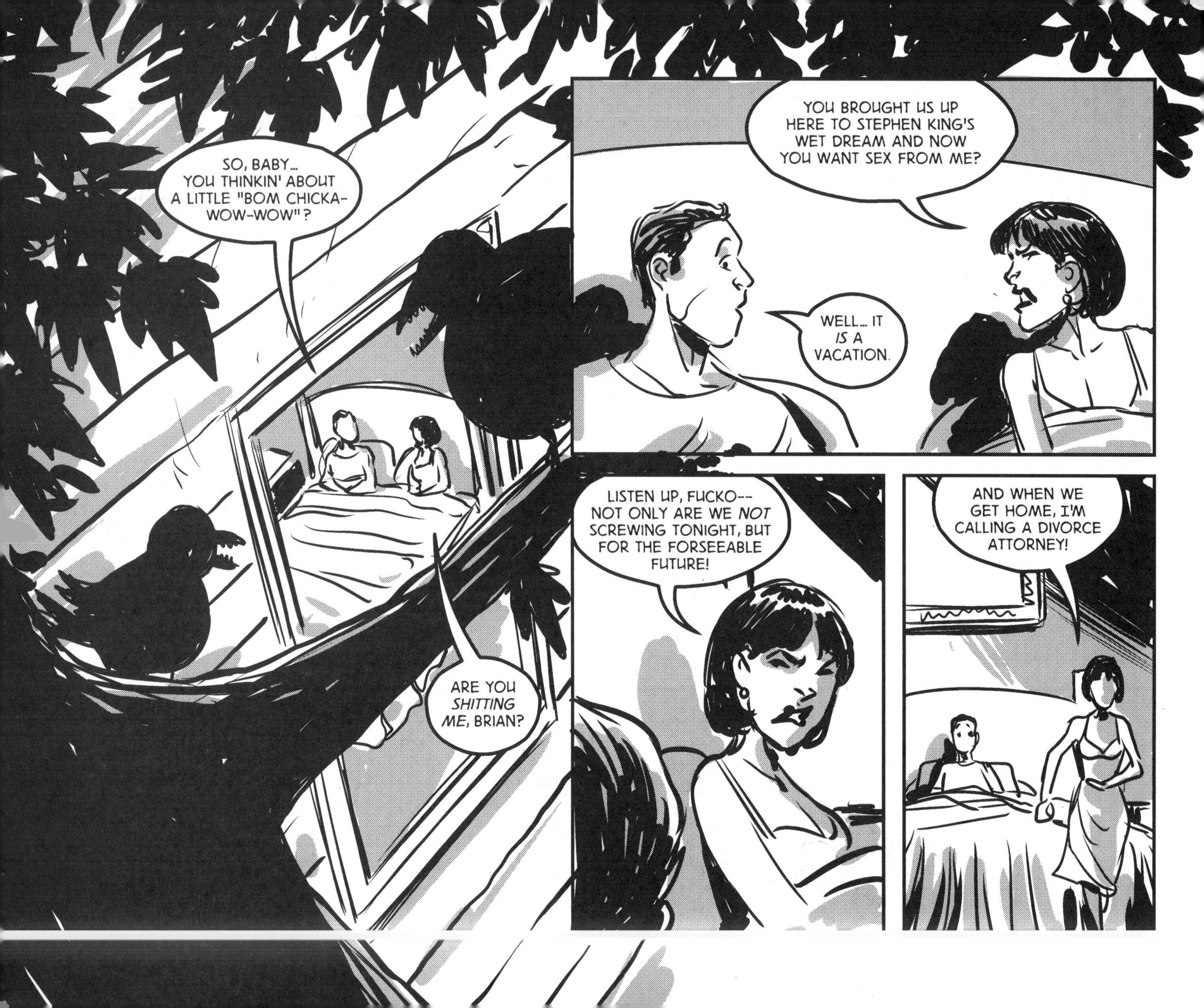
SO, BABY... YOU THINKIN' ABOUT A LITTLE "BOM CHICKA-WOW-WOW"?
ARE YOU *SHITTING ME*, BRIAN?
YOU BROUGHT US UP HERE TO STEPHEN KING'S WET DREAM AND NOW YOU WANT SEX FROM ME?
WELL... IT *IS* A VACATION.
LISTEN UP, FUCKO-- NOT ONLY ARE WE *NOT* SCREWING TONIGHT, BUT FOR THE FORSEEABLE FUTURE!
AND WHEN WE GET HOME, I'M CALLING A DIVORCE ATTORNEY!

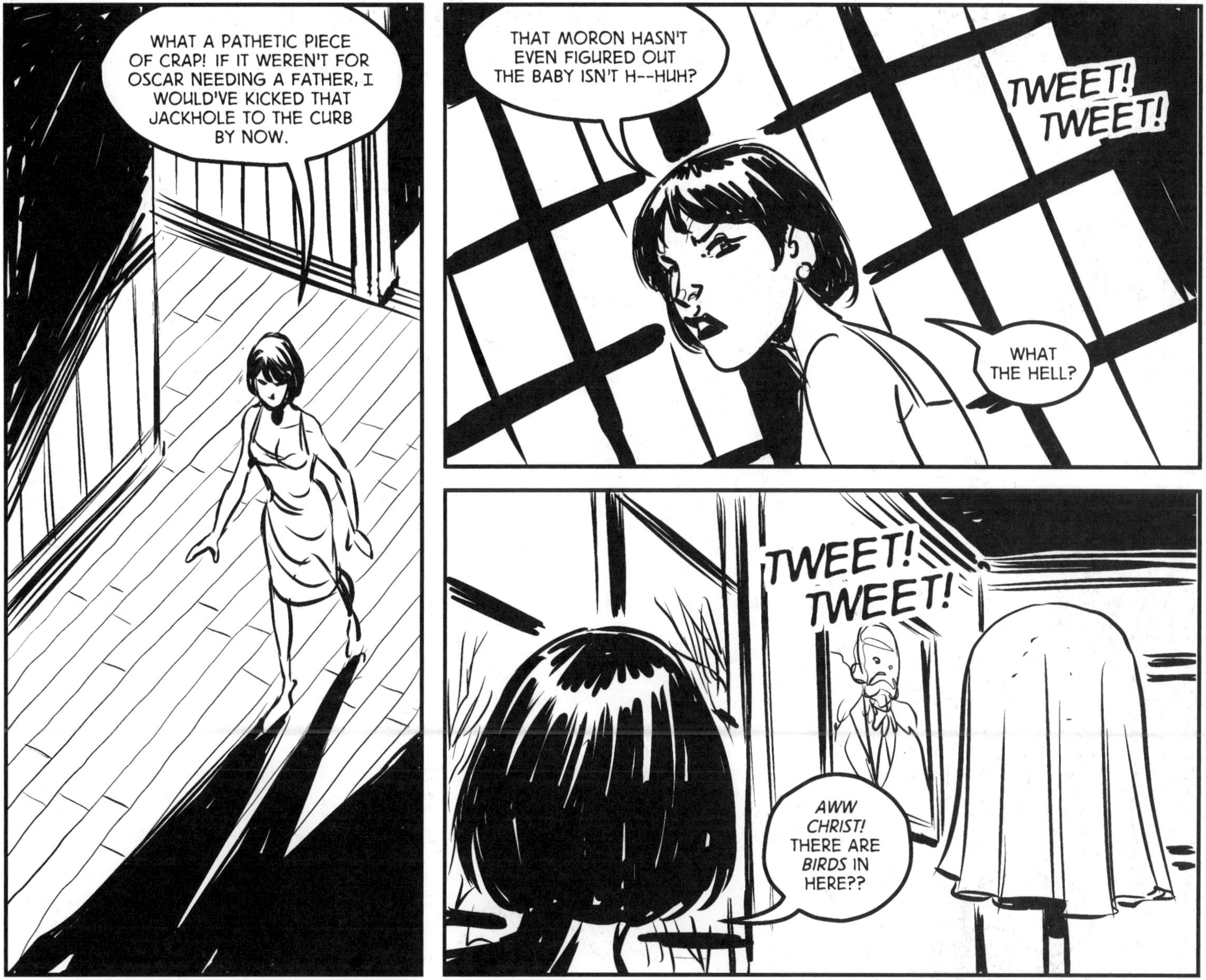
WHAT A PATHETIC PIECE OF CRAP! IF IT WEREN'T FOR OSCAR NEEDING A FATHER, I WOULD'VE KICKED THAT JACKHOLE TO THE CURB BY NOW.
THAT MORON HASN'T EVEN FIGURED OUT THE BABY ISN'T H--HUH?
TWEET! TWEET!
WHAT THE HELL?
TWEET! TWEET!
AWW CHRIST! THERE ARE *BIRDS* IN HERE??

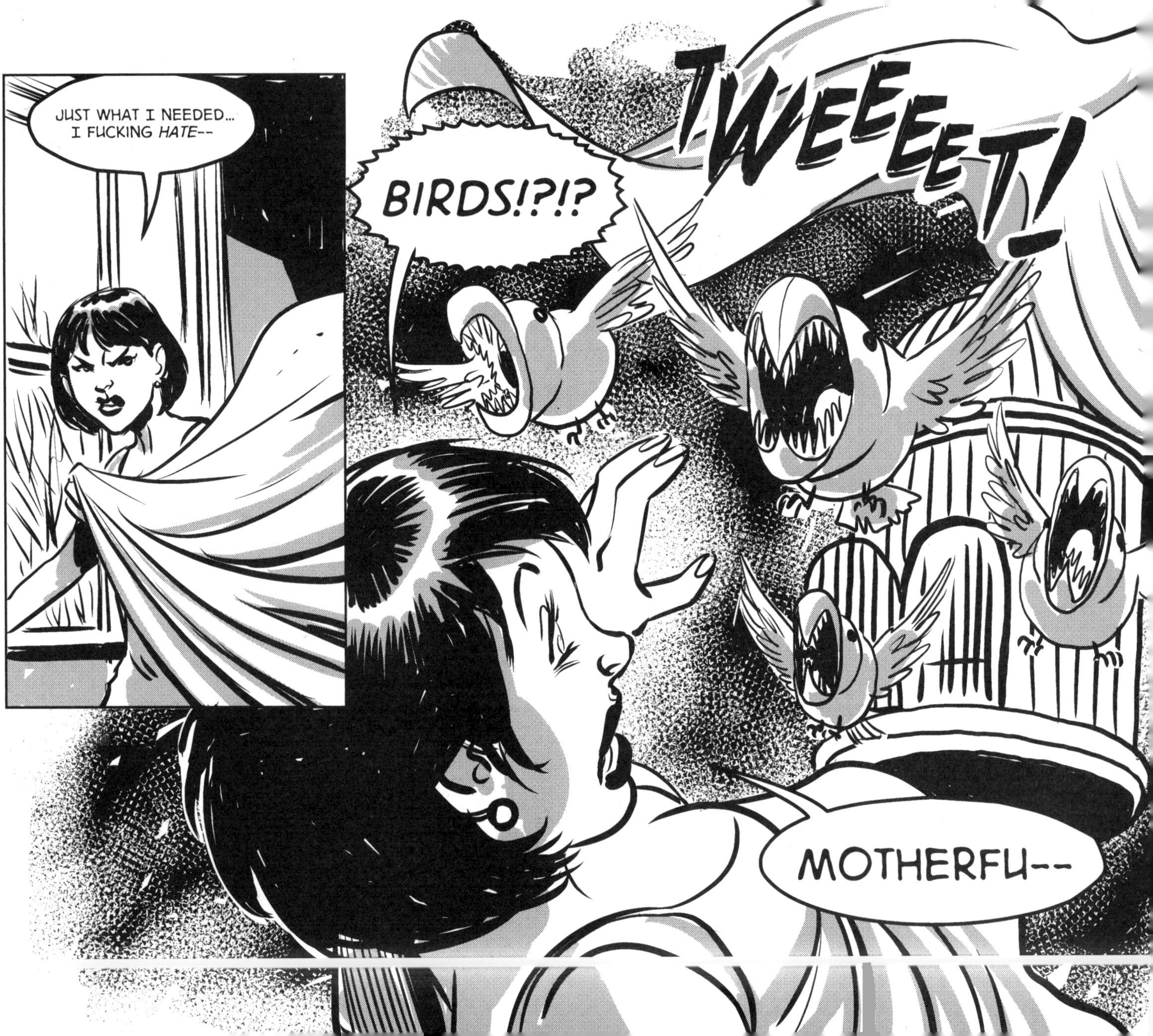
JUST WHAT I NEEDED...
I FUCKING HATE--
BIRDS!?!?
TWEEEEET!
MOTHERFU--

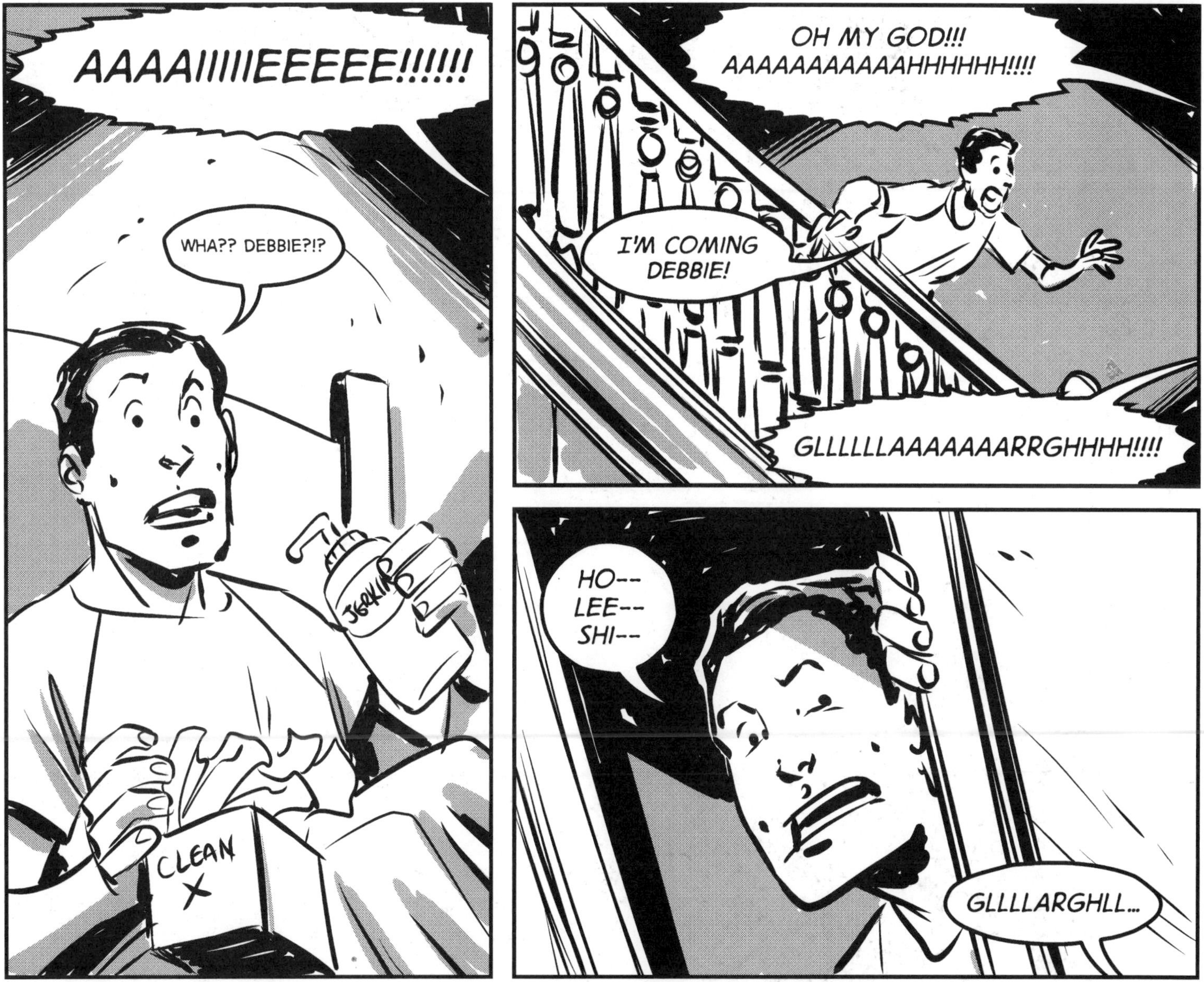
AAAAIIIIIEEEEE!!!!!!
WHA?? DEBBIE?!?
JERKIN
CLEAN
X
OH MY GOD!!!
AAAAAAAAAAAHHHHHH!!!!
I'M COMING DEBBIE!
GLLLLLLAAAAAAARRGHHHH!!!!
HO--
LEE--
SHI--
GLLLLARGHLL...

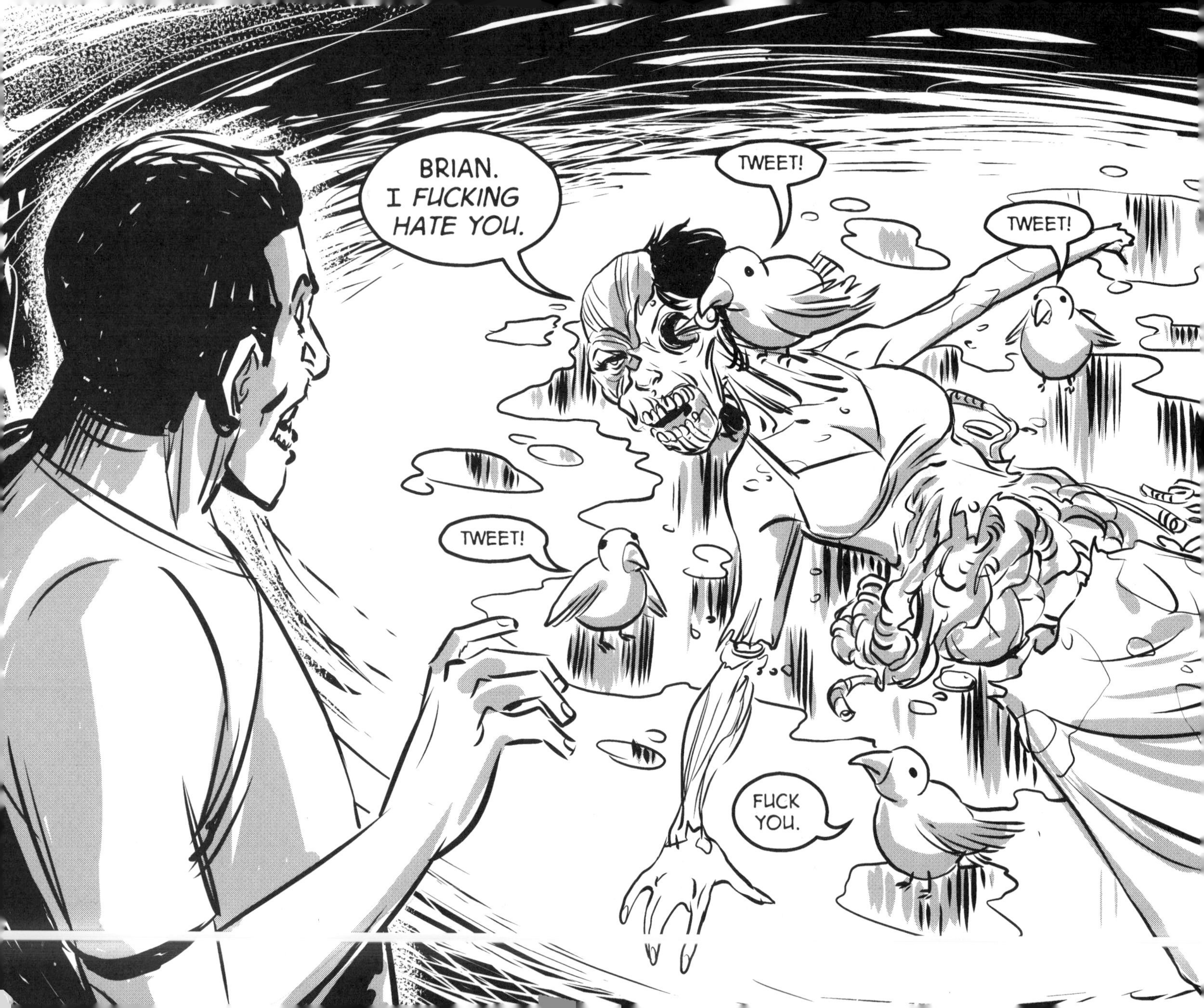
BRIAN. I *FUCKING* HATE YOU.
TWEET!
TWEET!
TWEET!
FUCK YOU.

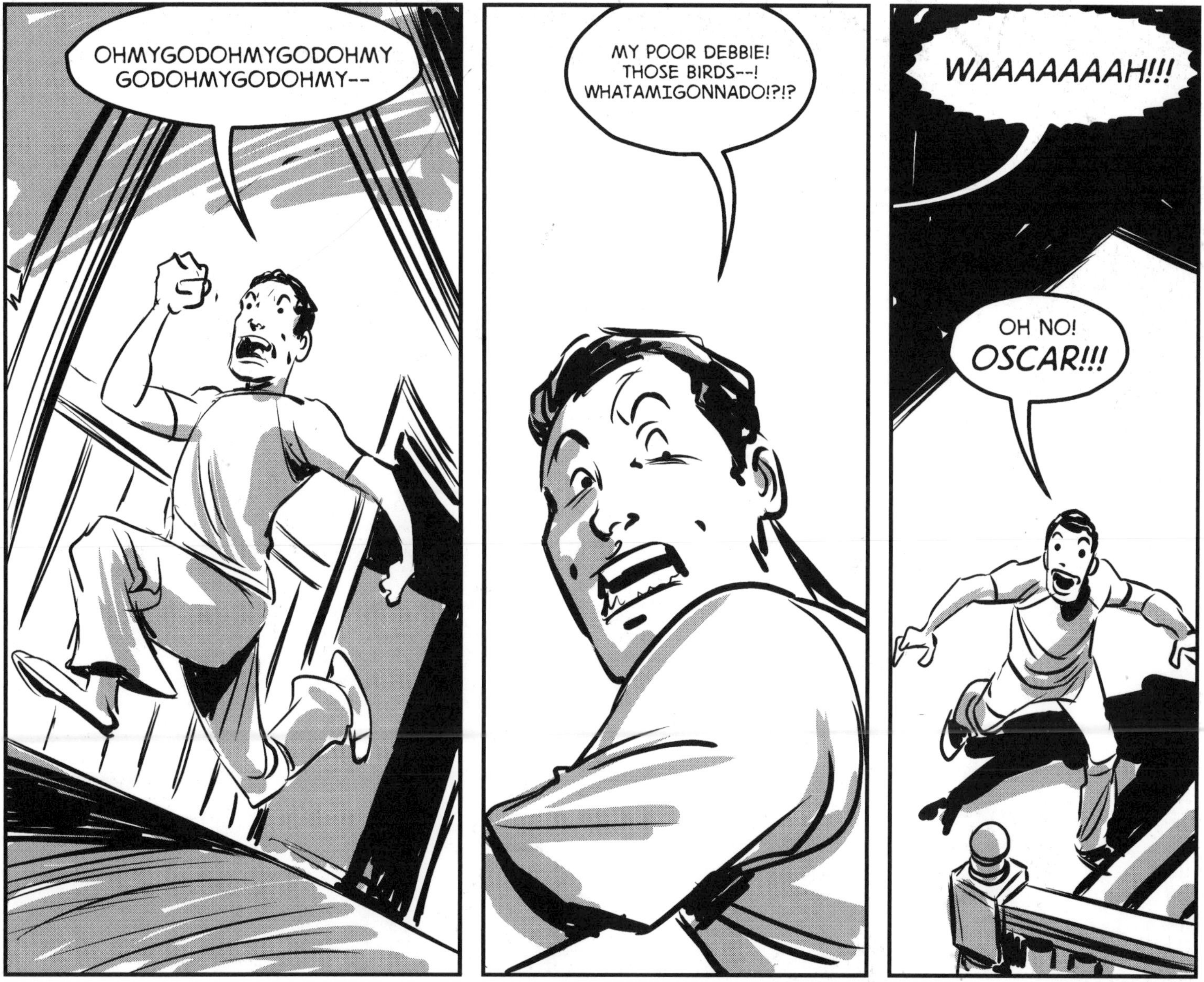
OHMYGODOHMYGODOHMY GODOHMYGODOHMY--
MY POOR DEBBIE! THOSE BIRDS--! WHATAMIGONNADO!?!?
WAAAAAAAH!!!
OH NO! OSCAR!!!

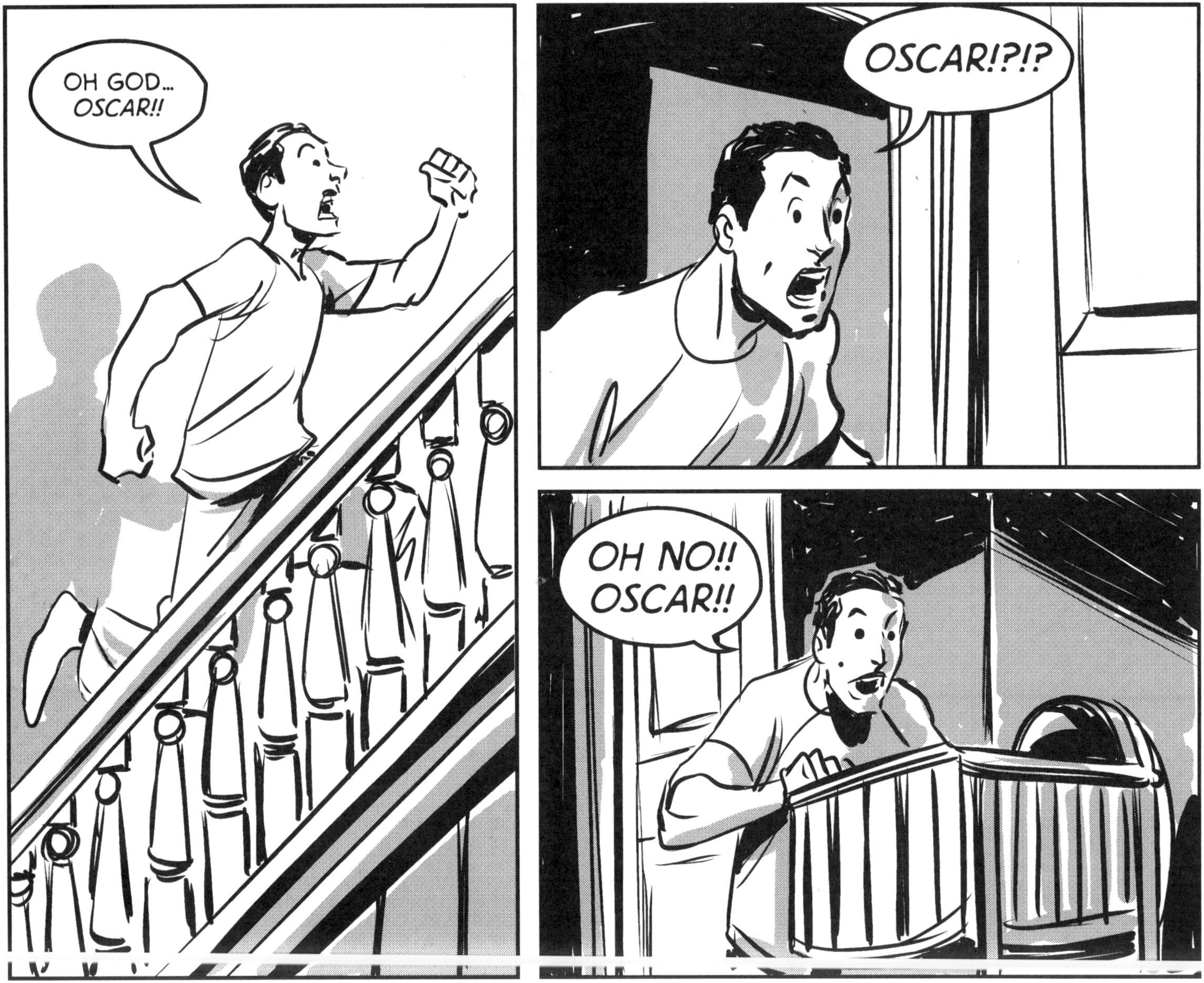
OH GOD... OSCAR!!
OSCAR!?!?
OH NO!! OSCAR!!

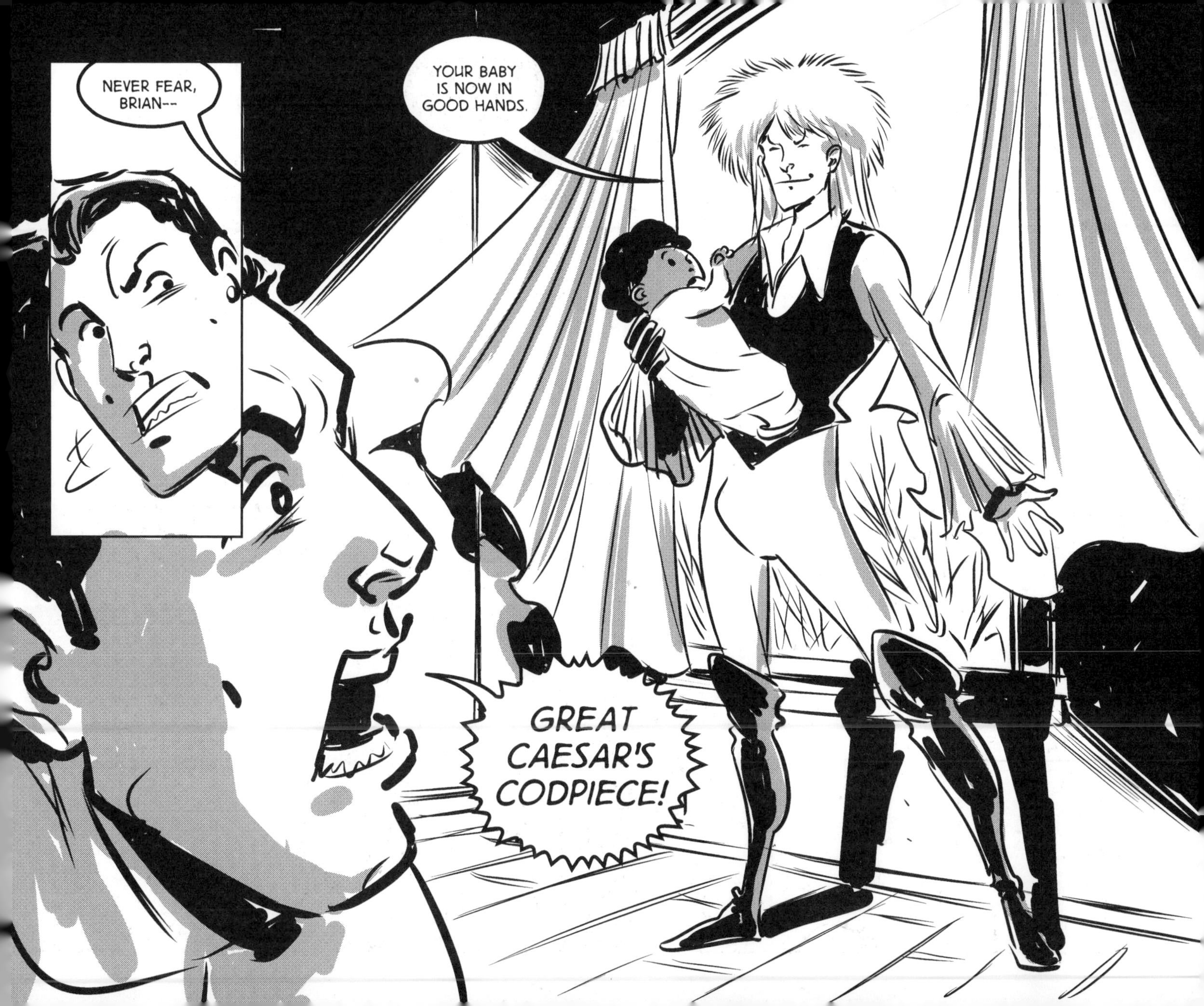
NEVER FEAR, BRIAN--
YOUR BABY IS NOW IN GOOD HANDS.
GREAT CAESAR'S CODPIECE!

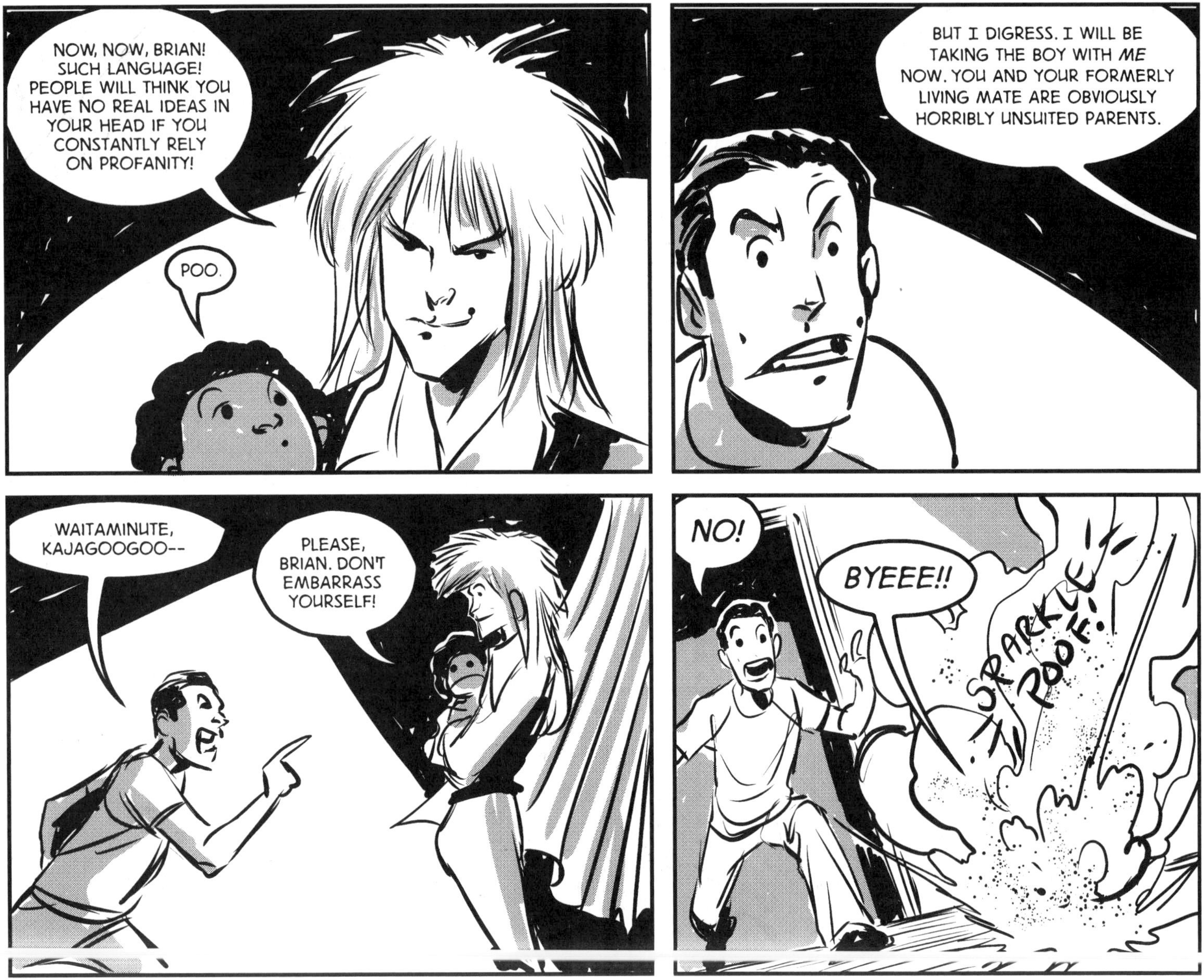
NOW, NOW, BRIAN! SUCH LANGUAGE! PEOPLE WILL THINK YOU HAVE NO REAL IDEAS IN YOUR HEAD IF YOU CONSTANTLY RELY ON PROFANITY!
POO.
BUT I DIGRESS. I WILL BE TAKING THE BOY WITH *ME* NOW. YOU AND YOUR FORMERLY LIVING MATE ARE OBVIOUSLY HORRIBLY UNSUITED PARENTS.
WAITAMINUTE, KAJAGOOGOO--
PLEASE, BRIAN. DON'T EMBARRASS YOURSELF!
NO!
BYEEE!!
SPARKLE POOF!

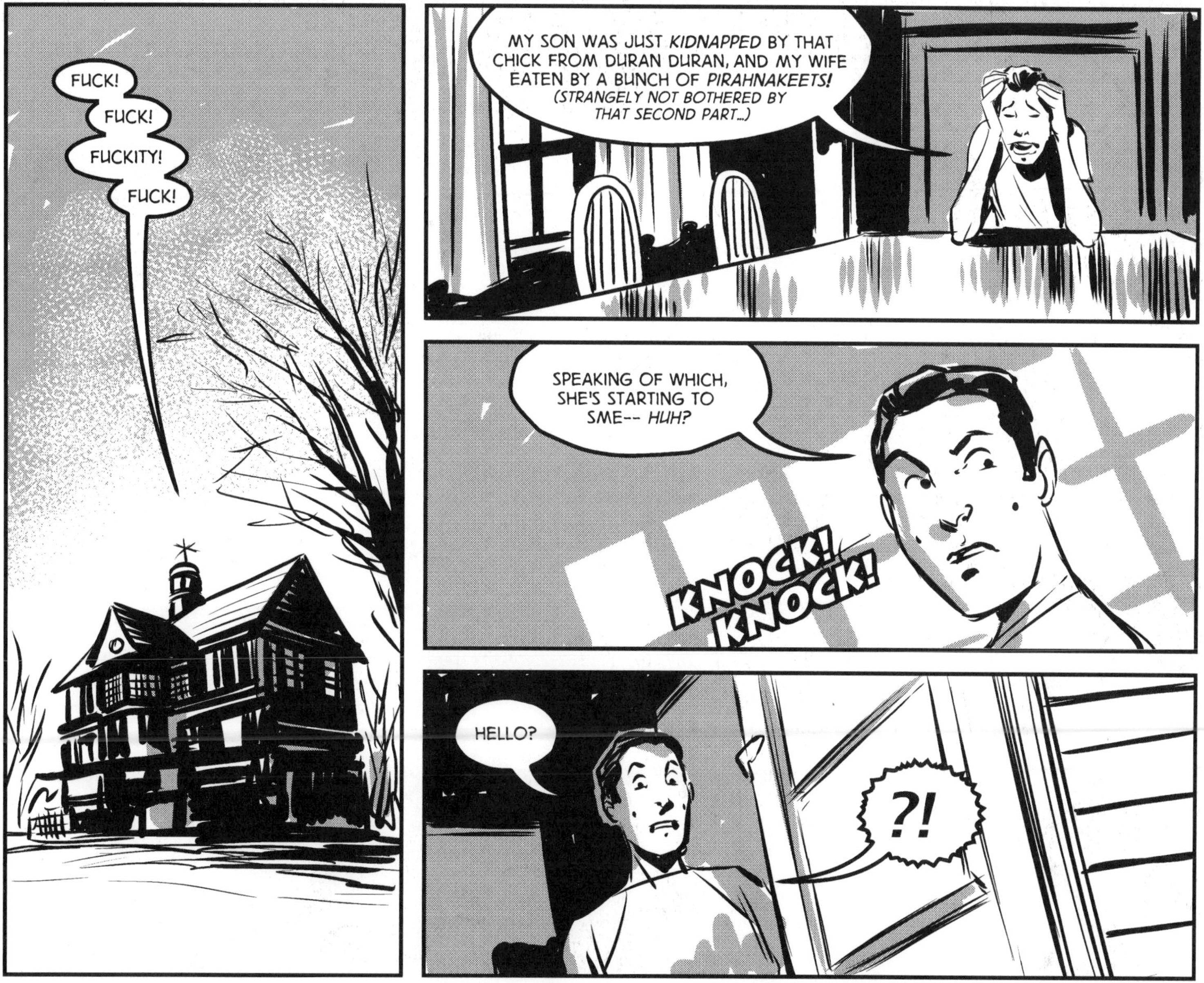

FUCK!
FUCK!
FUCKITY!
FUCK!
MY SON WAS JUST *KIDNAPPED* BY THAT CHICK FROM DURAN DURAN, AND MY WIFE EATEN BY A BUNCH OF *PIRAHNAKEETS!*
(STRANGELY NOT BOTHERED BY THAT SECOND PART...)
SPEAKING OF WHICH, SHE'S STARTING TO SME-- *HUH?*
KNOCK! KNOCK!
HELLO?
?!

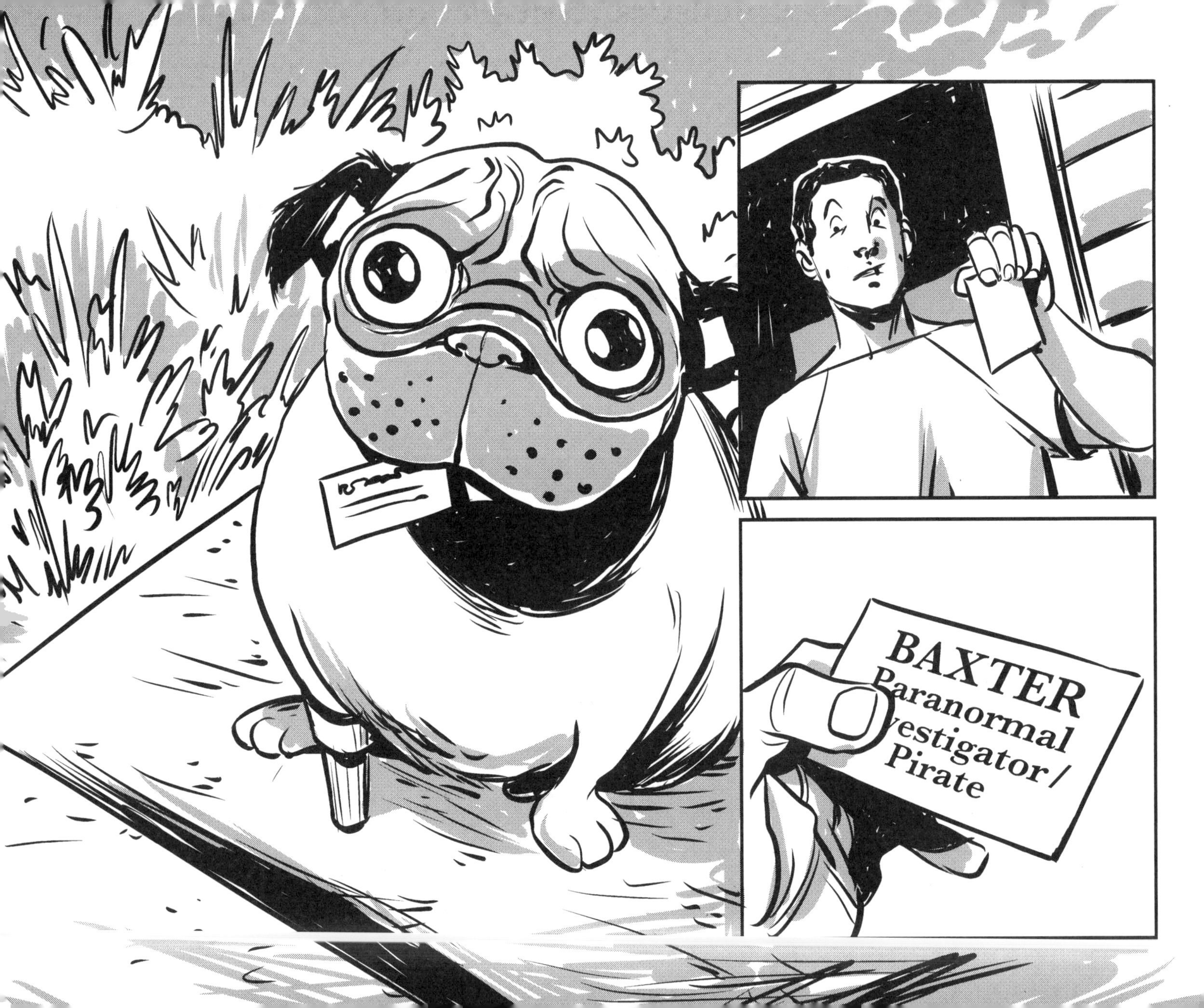
BAXTER
Paranormal
vestigator/
Pirate

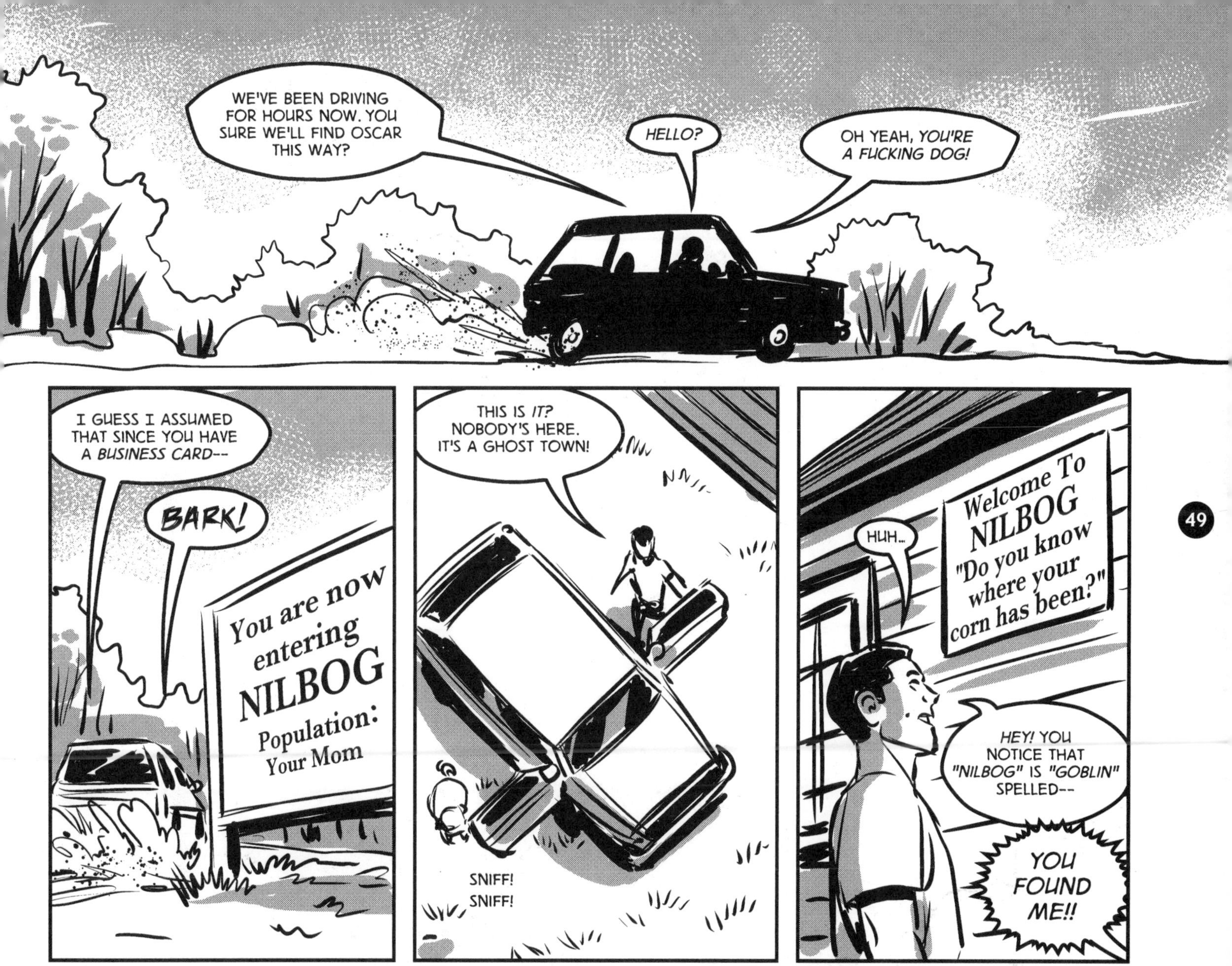
WE'VE BEEN DRIVING FOR HOURS NOW. YOU SURE WE'LL FIND OSCAR THIS WAY?
HELLO?
OH YEAH, *YOU'RE A FUCKING DOG!*
I GUESS I ASSUMED THAT SINCE YOU HAVE A *BUSINESS CARD*--
BARK!
You are now entering NILBOG Population: Your Mom
THIS IS *IT?* NOBODY'S HERE. IT'S A GHOST TOWN!
SNIFF! SNIFF!
HUH...
Welcome To NILBOG "Do you know where your corn has been?"
HEY! YOU NOTICE THAT *"NILBOG"* IS *"GOBLIN"* SPELLED--
YOU FOUND ME!!

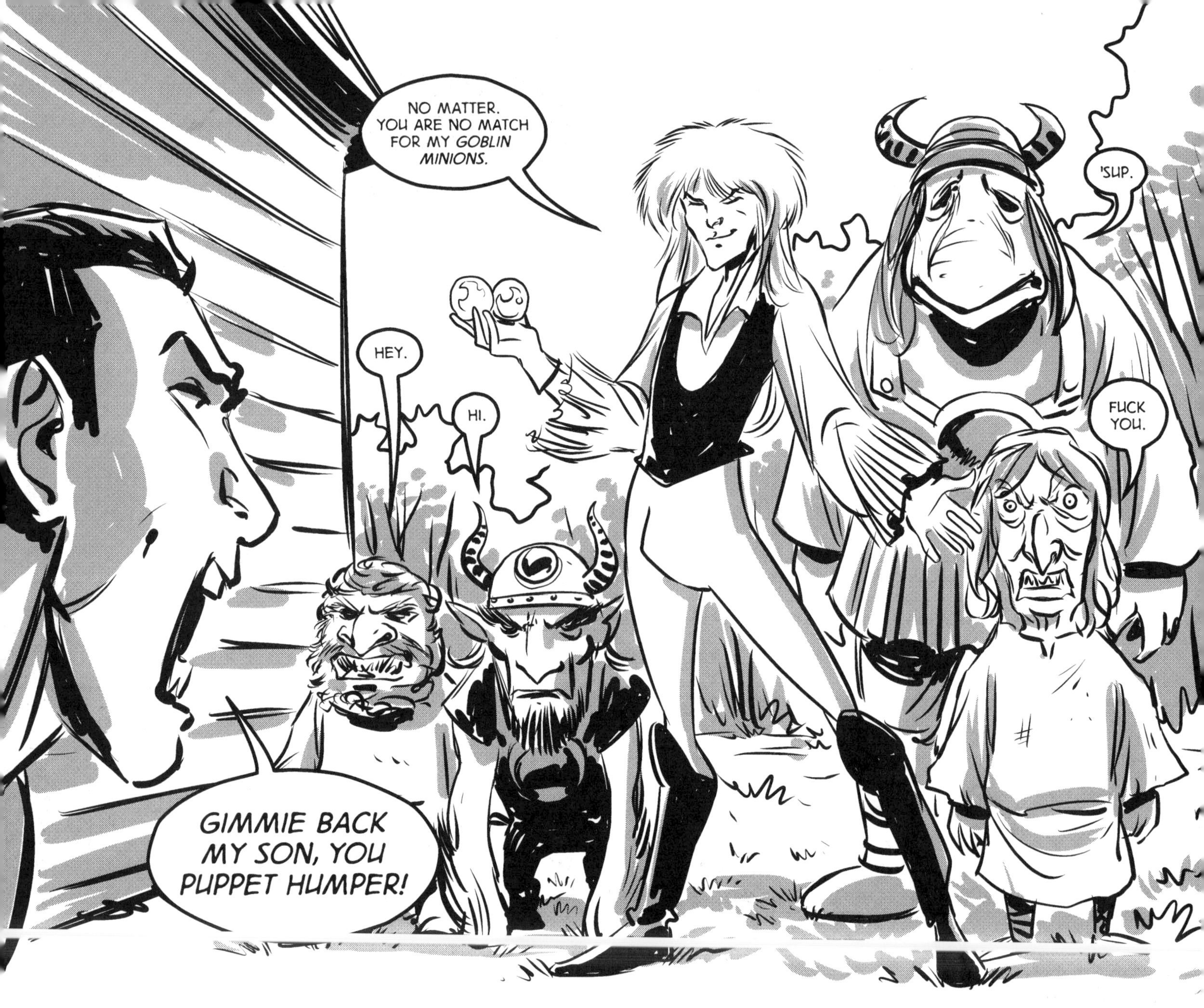
NO MATTER. YOU ARE NO MATCH FOR MY *GOBLIN MINIONS.*
'SUP.
HEY.
HI.
FUCK YOU.
GIMMIE BACK MY SON, YOU PUPPET HUMPER!

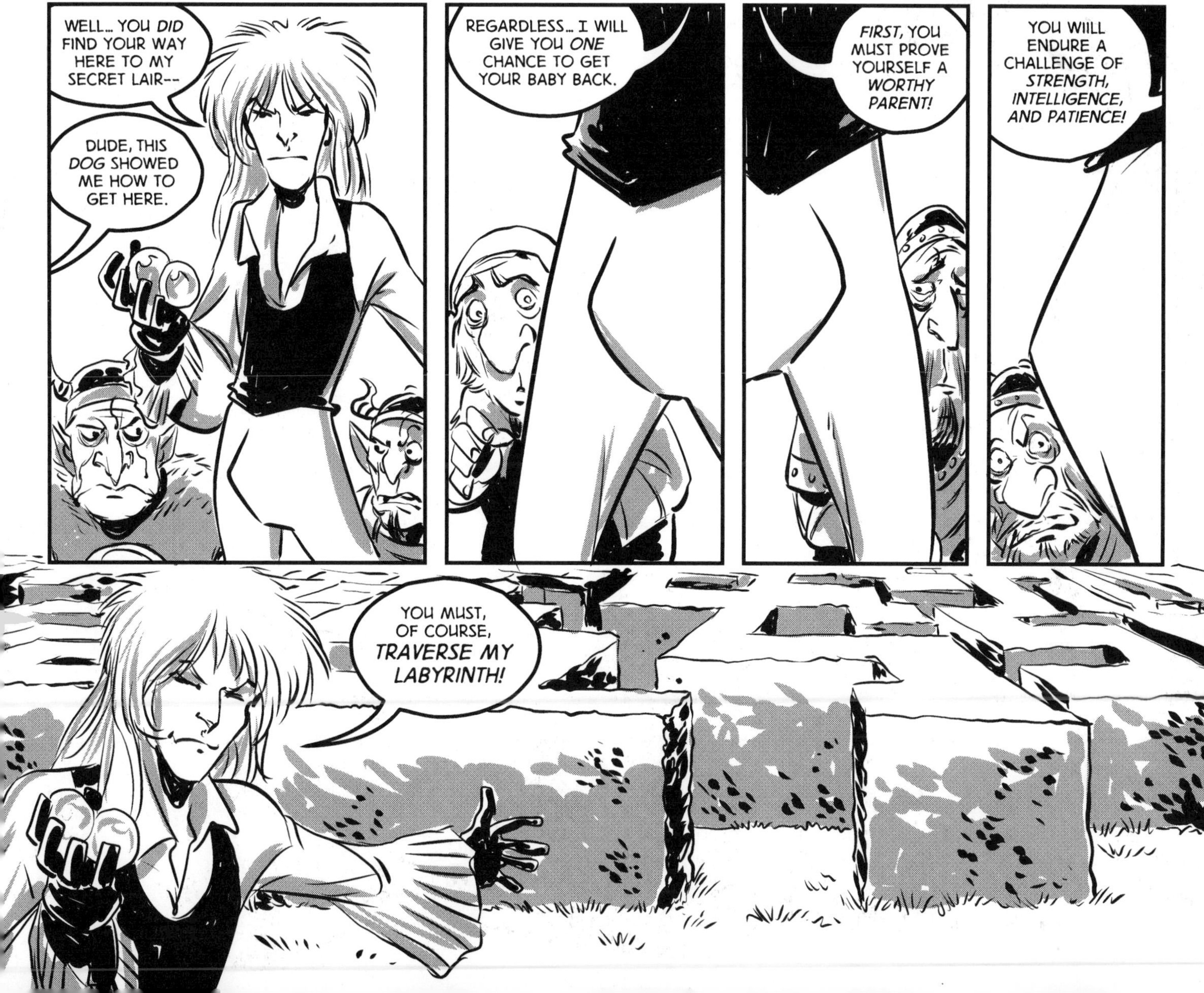
WELL... YOU *DID* FIND YOUR WAY HERE TO MY SECRET LAIR--
DUDE, THIS *DOG* SHOWED ME HOW TO GET HERE.
REGARDLESS... I WILL GIVE YOU *ONE* CHANCE TO GET YOUR BABY BACK.
FIRST, YOU MUST PROVE YOURSELF A *WORTHY PARENT!*
YOU WILL ENDURE A CHALLENGE OF *STRENGTH, INTELLIGENCE, AND PATIENCE!*
YOU MUST, OF COURSE, *TRAVERSE MY LABYRINTH!*

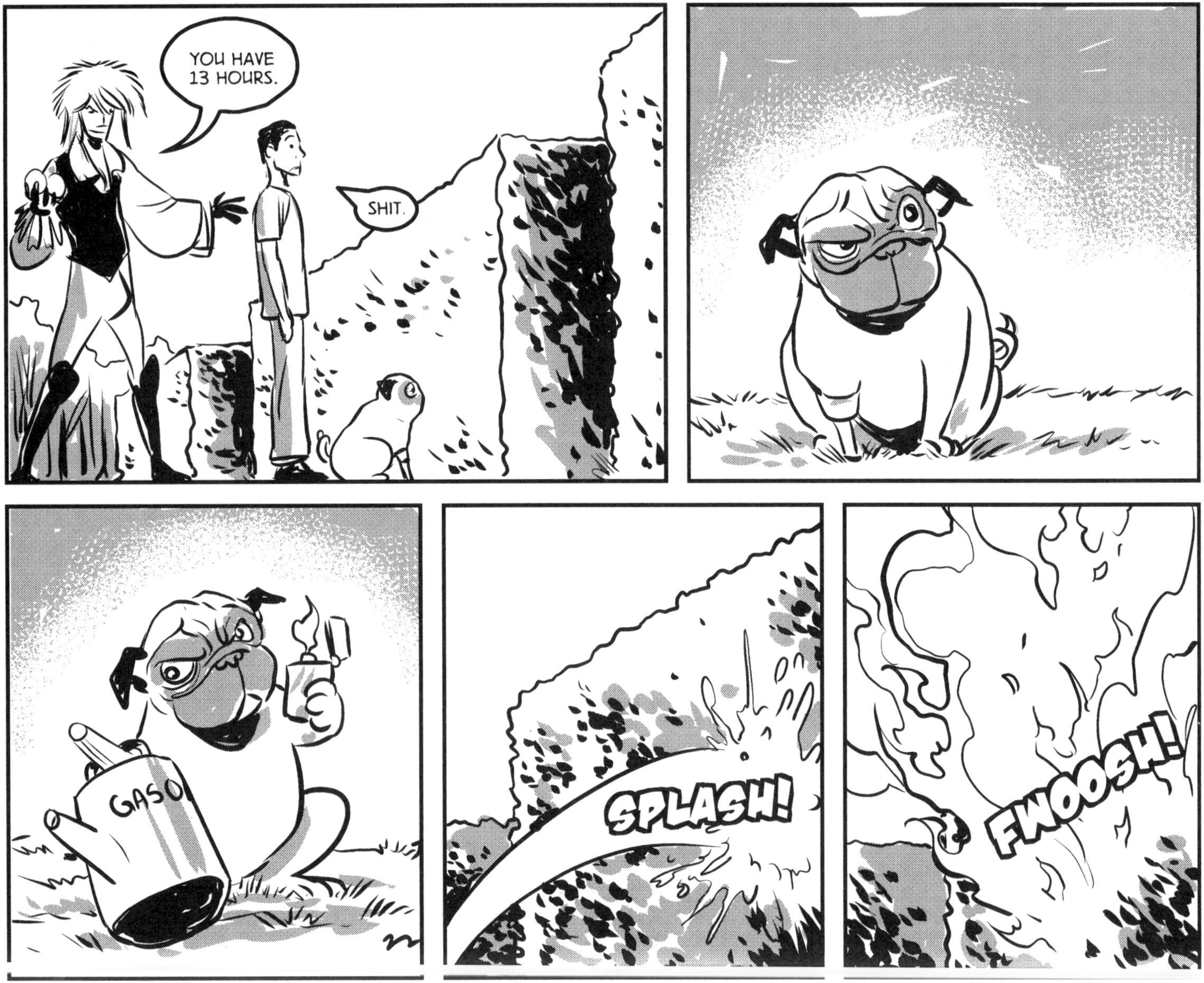
YOU HAVE 13 HOURS.
SHIT.
GASO
SPLASH!
FWOOSH!

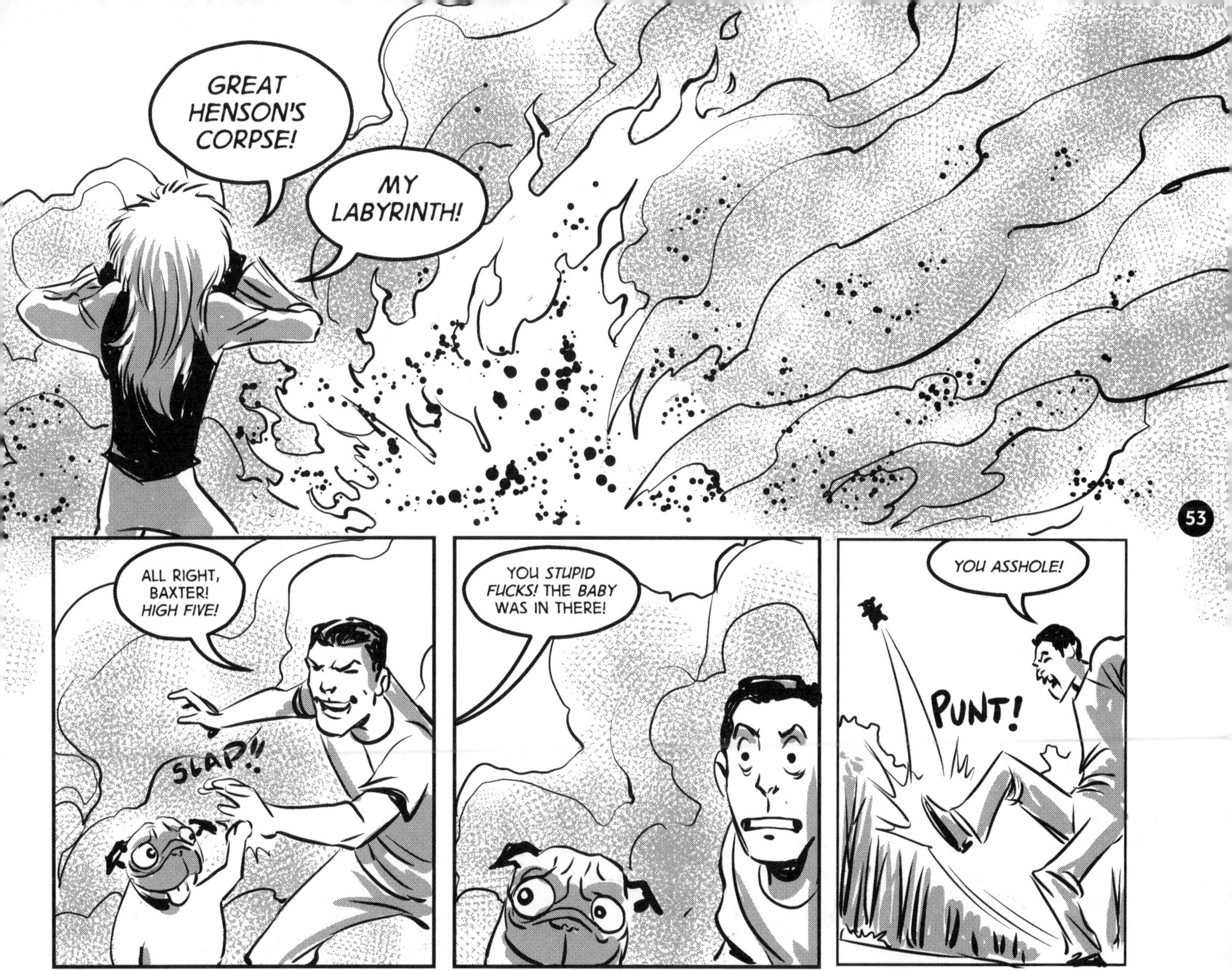
GREAT HENSON'S CORPSE!
MY LABYRINTH!
ALL RIGHT, BAXTER! HIGH FIVE!
SLAP!!
YOU STUPID FUCKS! THE BABY WAS IN THERE!
YOU ASSHOLE!
PUNT!

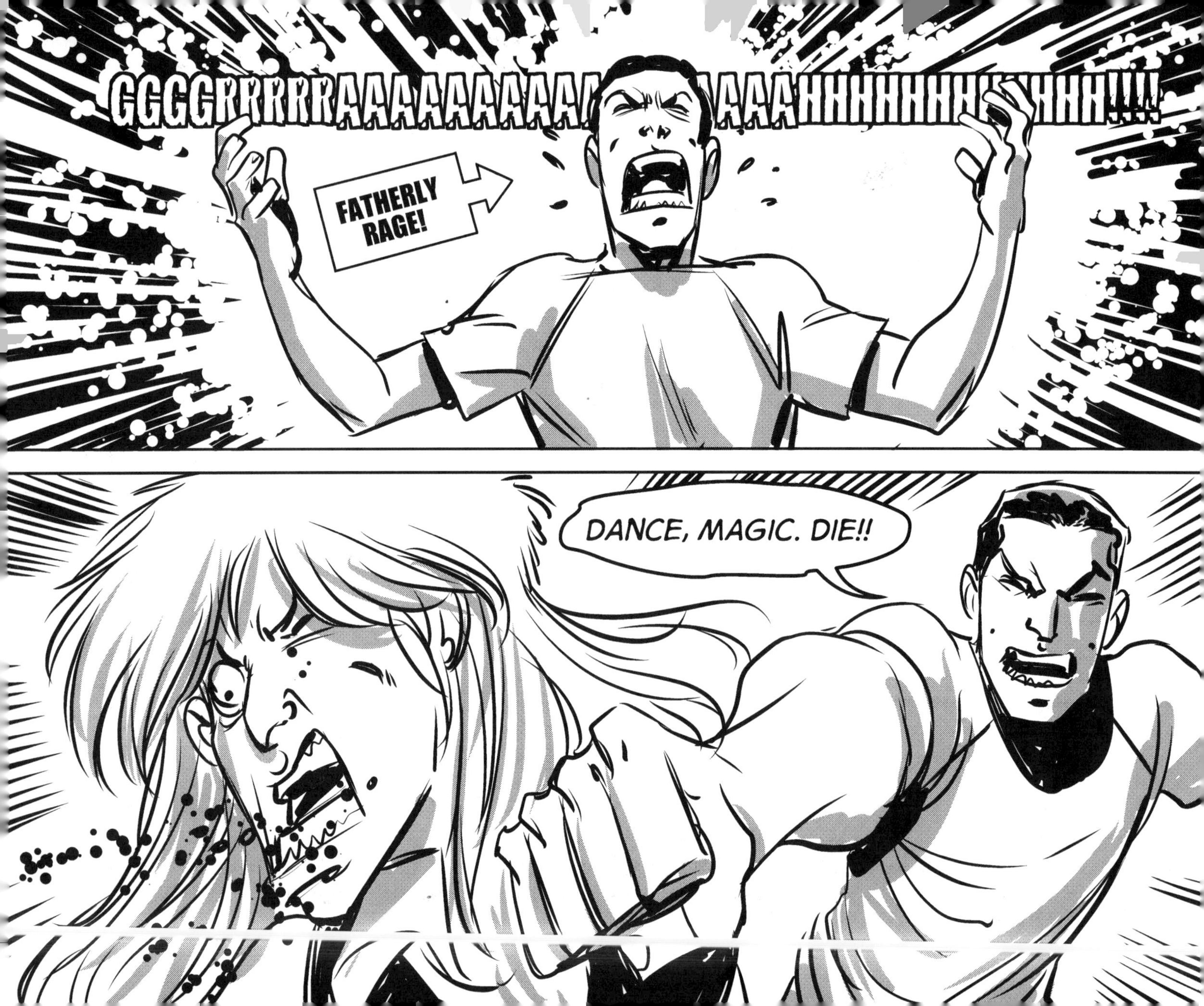
GGGGRRRRRAAAAAAAAAAAAAAAHHHHHHHHHHHH!!!!
FATHERLY RAGE!
DANCE, MAGIC. DIE!!

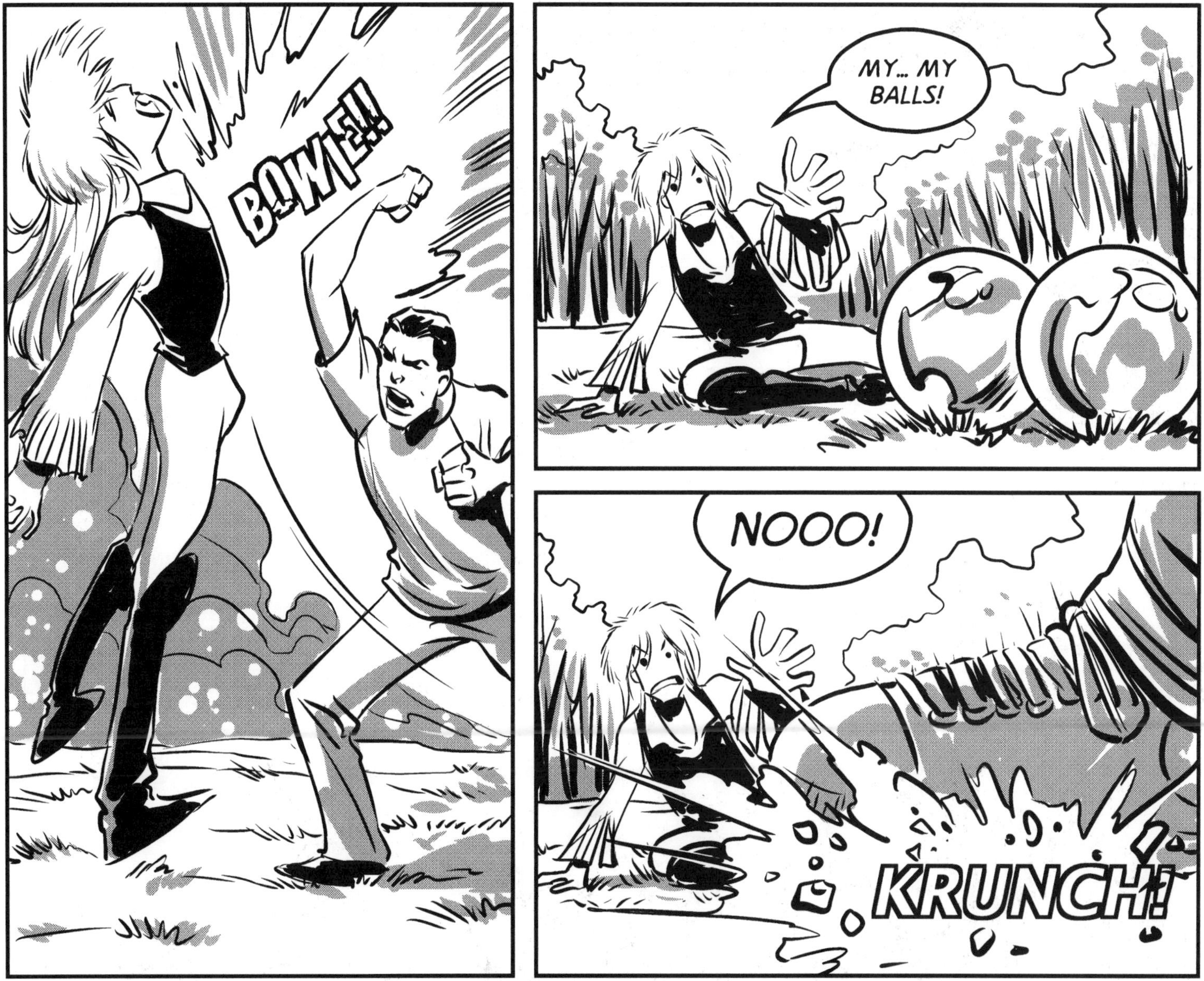
BOWIE!!
MY... MY BALLS!
NOOO!
KRUNCH!

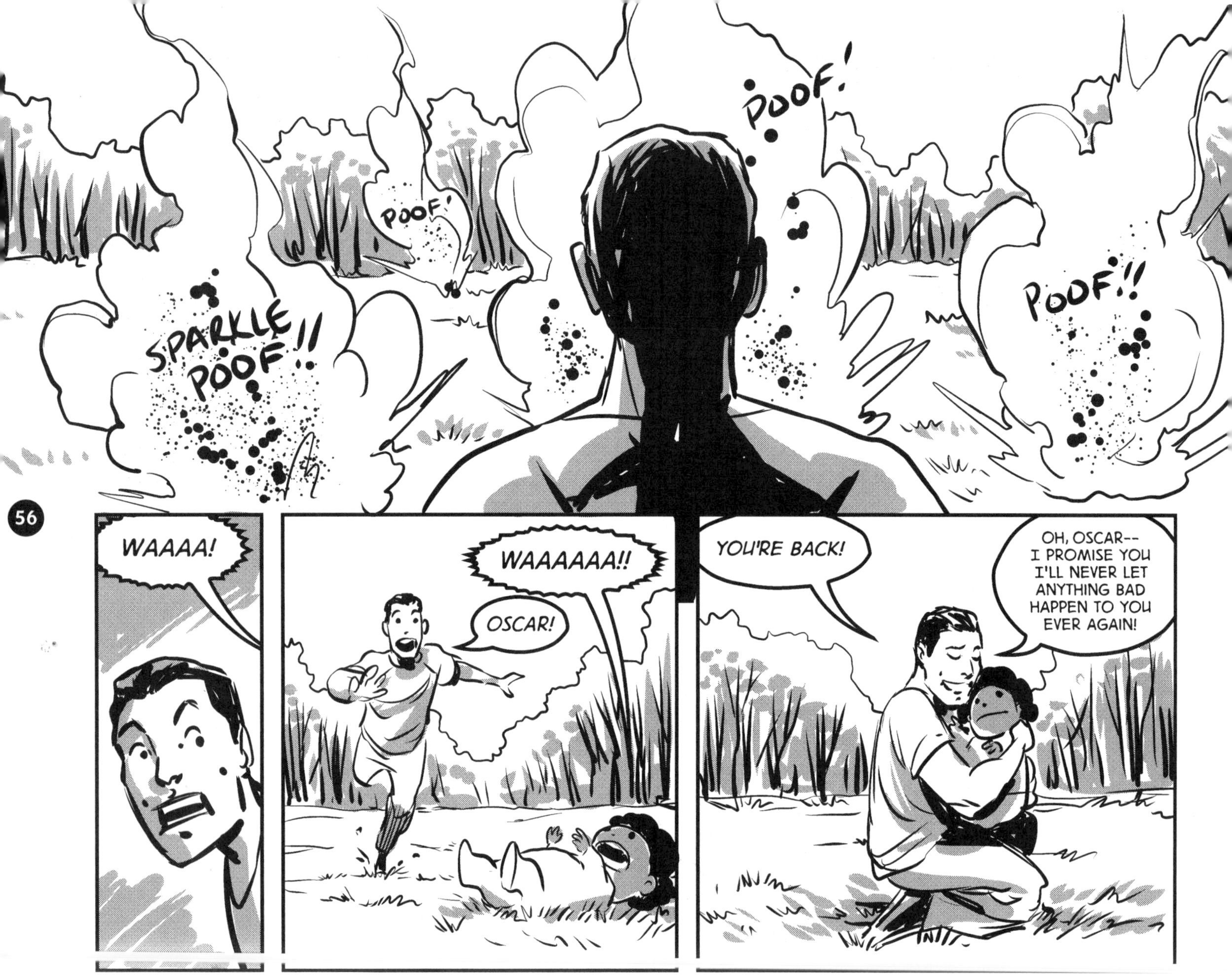
SPARKLE POOF!!
POOF!
POOF!
POOF!!
WAAAA!
WAAAAAA!!
OSCAR!
YOU'RE BACK!
OH, OSCAR-- I PROMISE YOU I'LL NEVER LET ANYTHING BAD HAPPEN TO YOU EVER AGAIN!

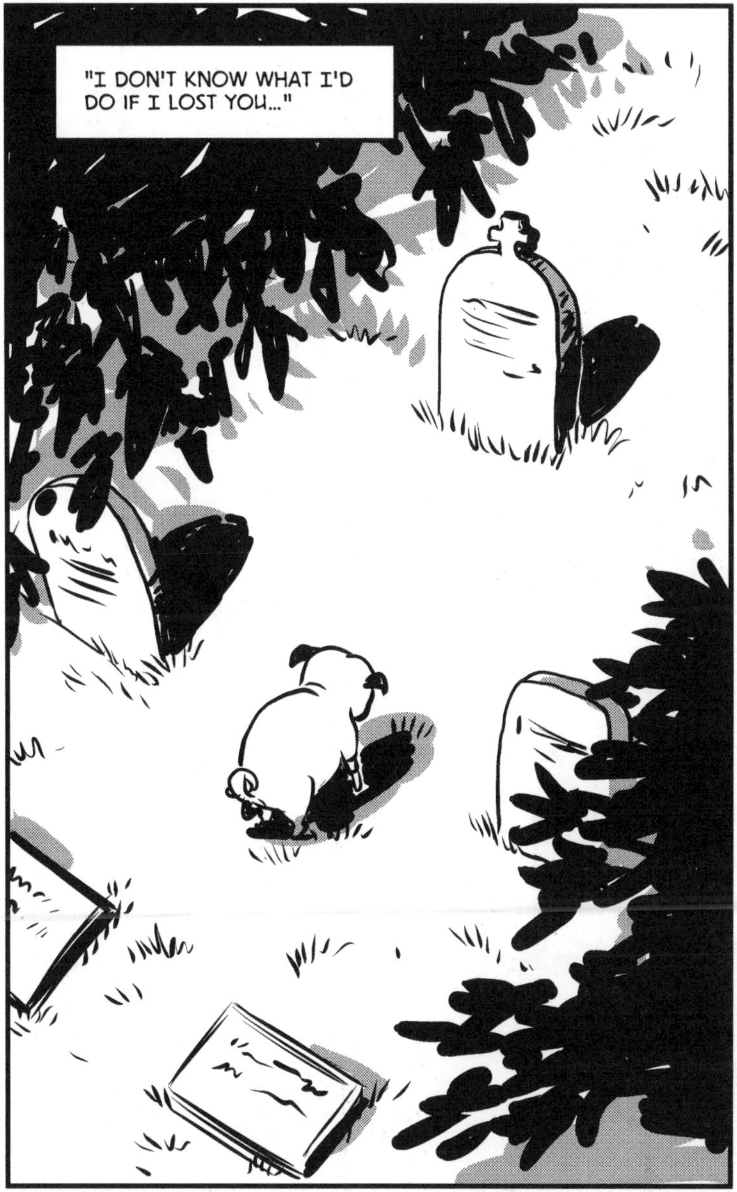
"I DON'T KNOW WHAT I'D DO IF I LOST YOU..."

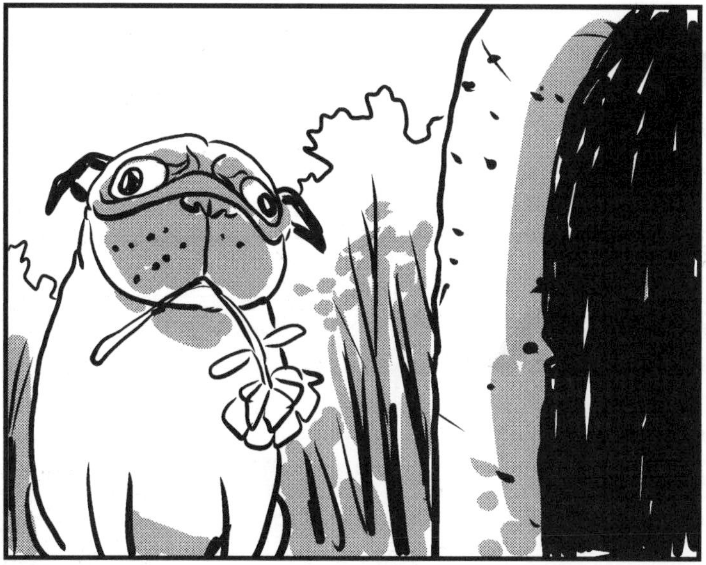

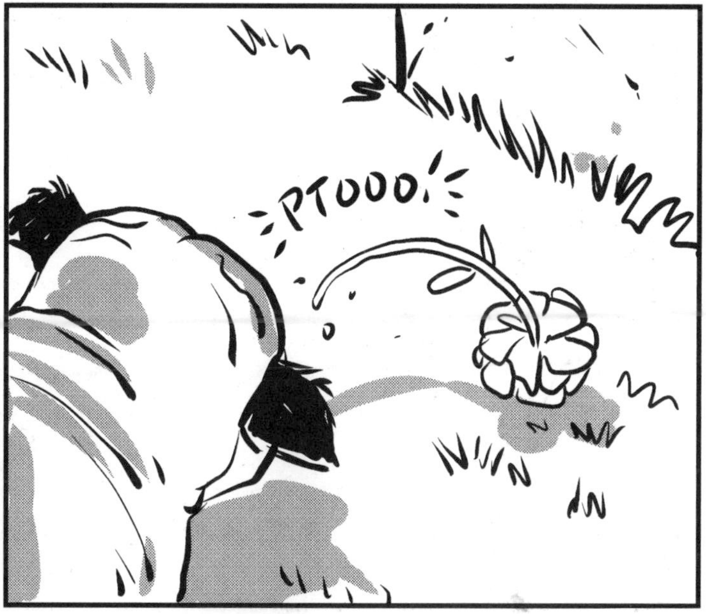
PTOOO!

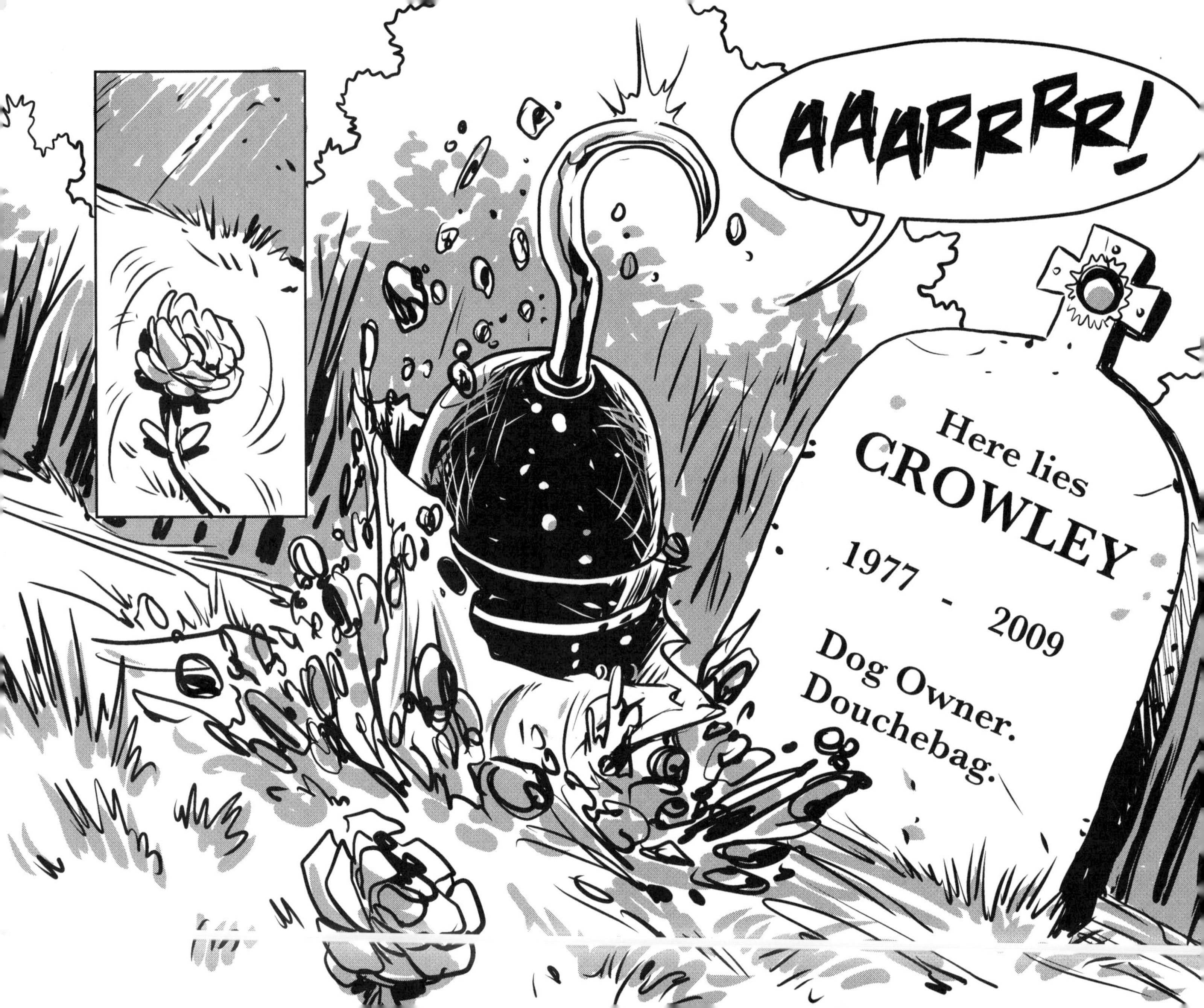
AAARRRR!
Here lies
CROWLEY
1977 - 2009
Dog Owner.
Douchebag.

THE CURSE 3.0

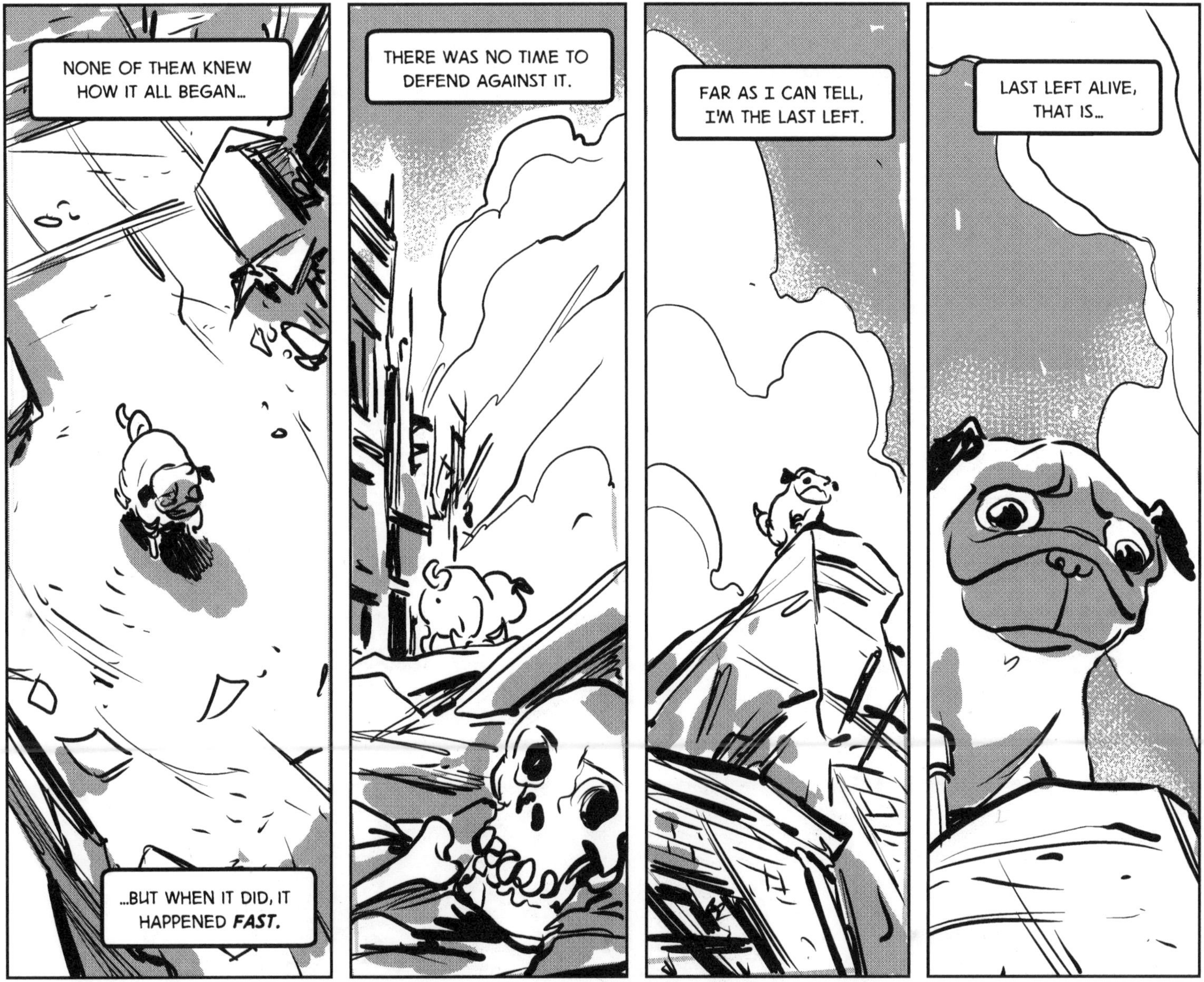
NONE OF THEM KNEW HOW IT ALL BEGAN...
...BUT WHEN IT DID, IT HAPPENED *FAST.*
THERE WAS NO TIME TO DEFEND AGAINST IT.
FAR AS I CAN TELL, I'M THE LAST LEFT.
LAST LEFT ALIVE, THAT IS...

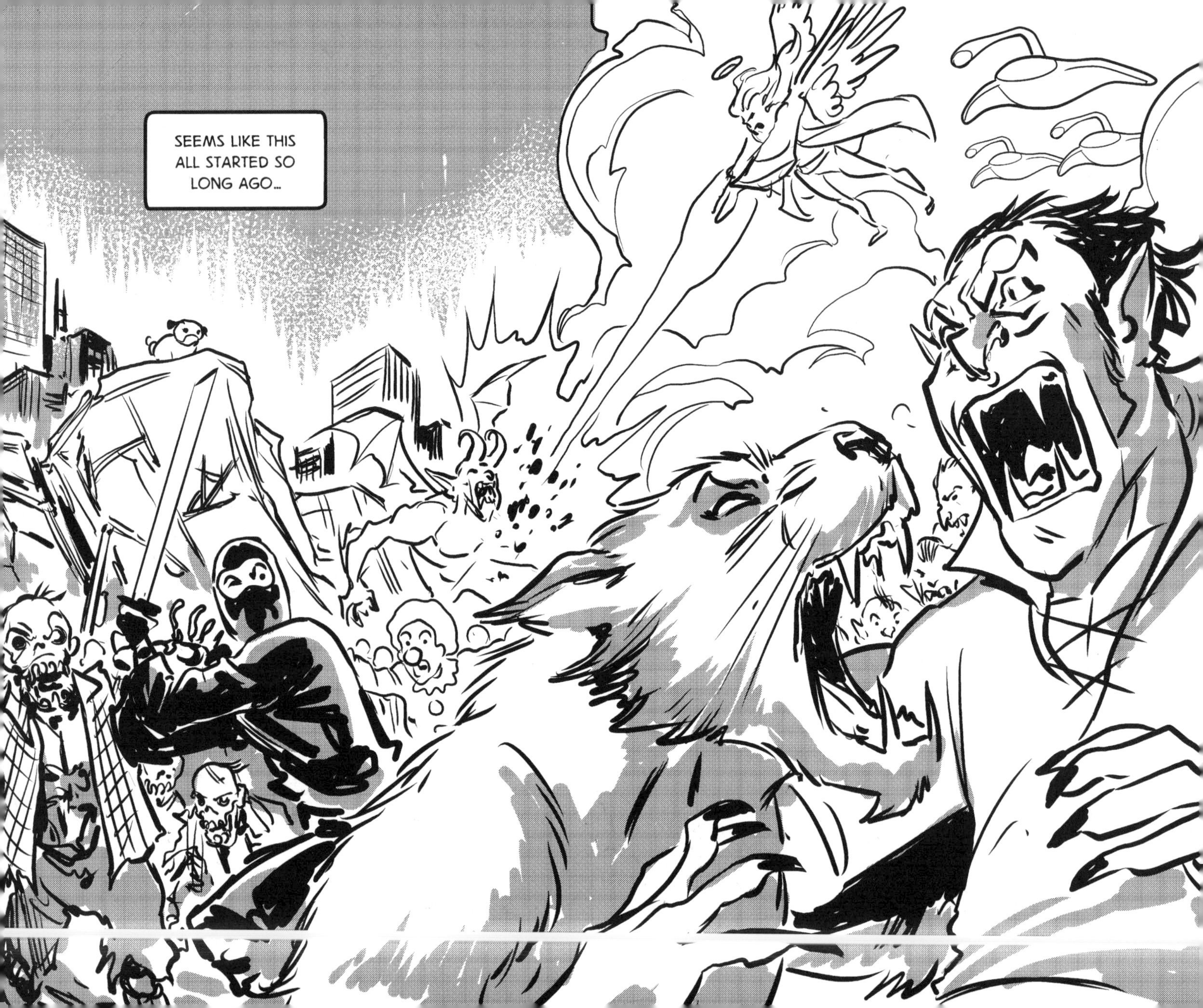
SEEMS LIKE THIS ALL STARTED SO LONG AGO...

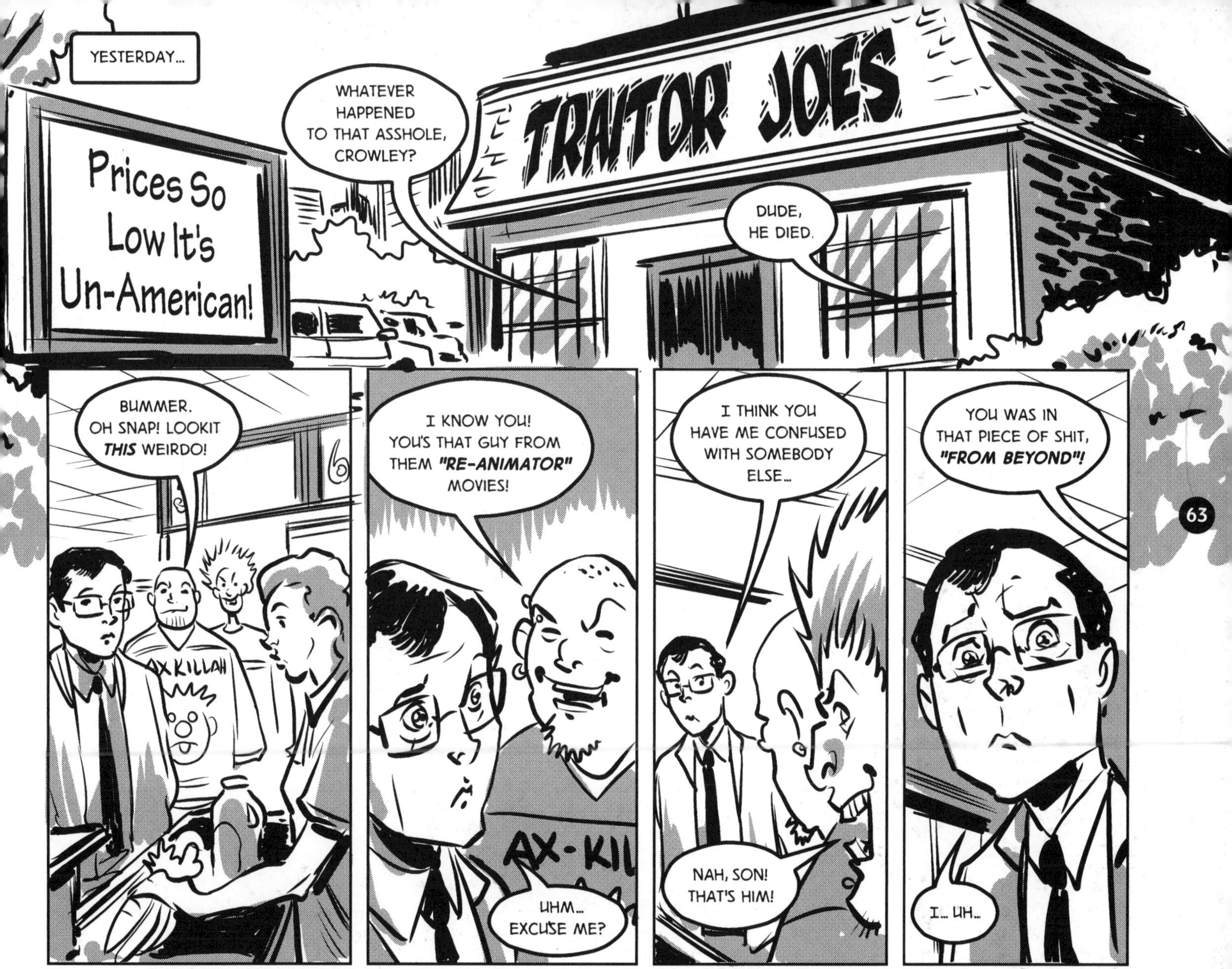

YESTERDAY...
Prices So Low It's Un-American!
TRAITOR JOES
WHATEVER HAPPENED TO THAT ASSHOLE, CROWLEY?
DUDE, HE DIED.
BUMMER. OH SNAP! LOOKIT THIS WEIRDO!
AX KILLAH
I KNOW YOU! YOU'S THAT GUY FROM THEM "RE-ANIMATOR" MOVIES!
UHM... EXCUSE ME?
I THINK YOU HAVE ME CONFUSED WITH SOMEBODY ELSE...
NAH, SON! THAT'S HIM!
YOU WAS IN THAT PIECE OF SHIT, "FROM BEYOND"!
I... UH...

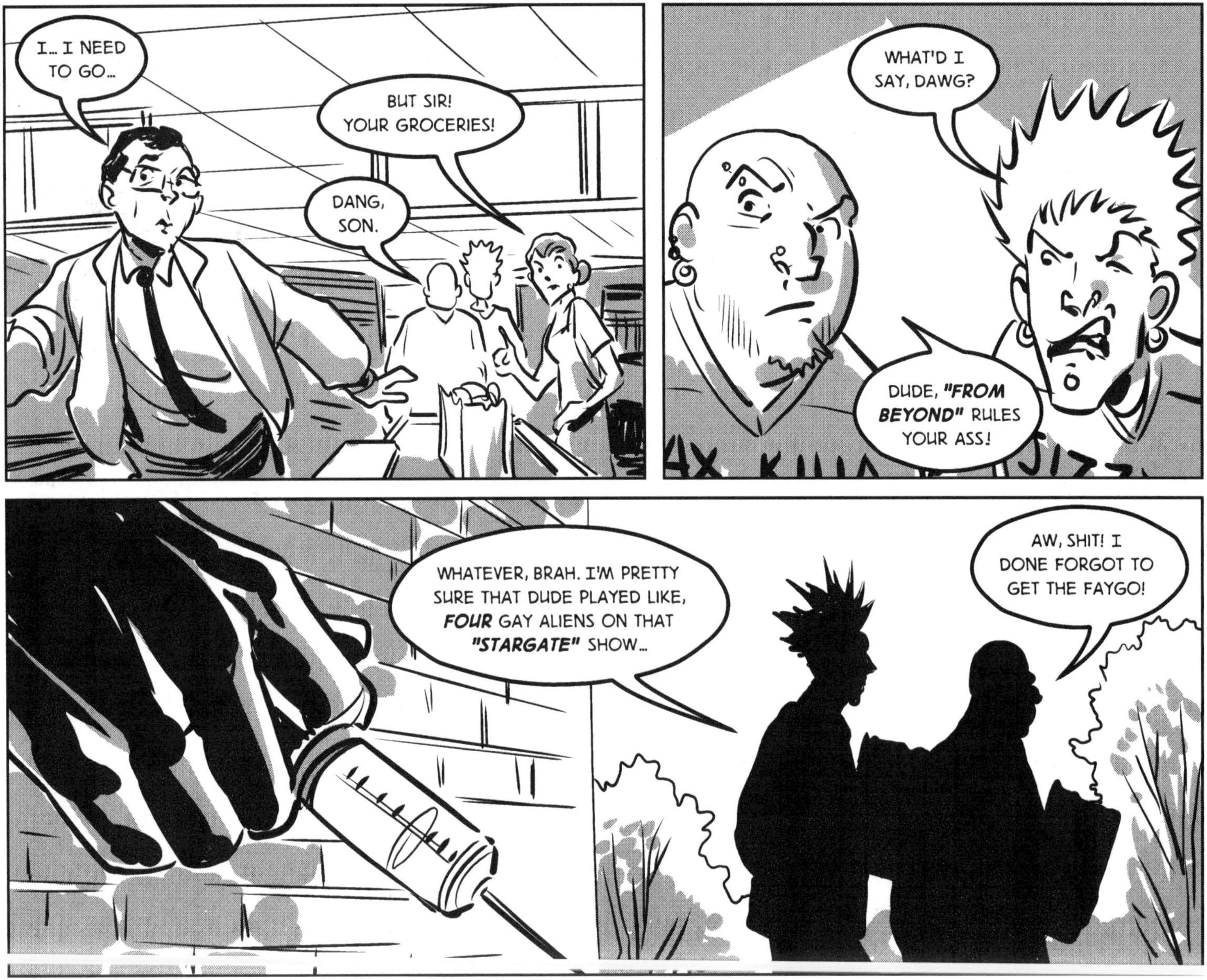
I... I NEED TO GO...
BUT SIR! YOUR GROCERIES!
DANG, SON.
WHAT'D I SAY, DAWG?
DUDE, **"FROM BEYOND"** RULES YOUR ASS!
WHATEVER, BRAH. I'M PRETTY SURE THAT DUDE PLAYED LIKE, ***FOUR*** GAY ALIENS ON THAT ***"STARGATE"*** SHOW...
AW, SHIT! I DONE FORGOT TO GET THE FAYGO!

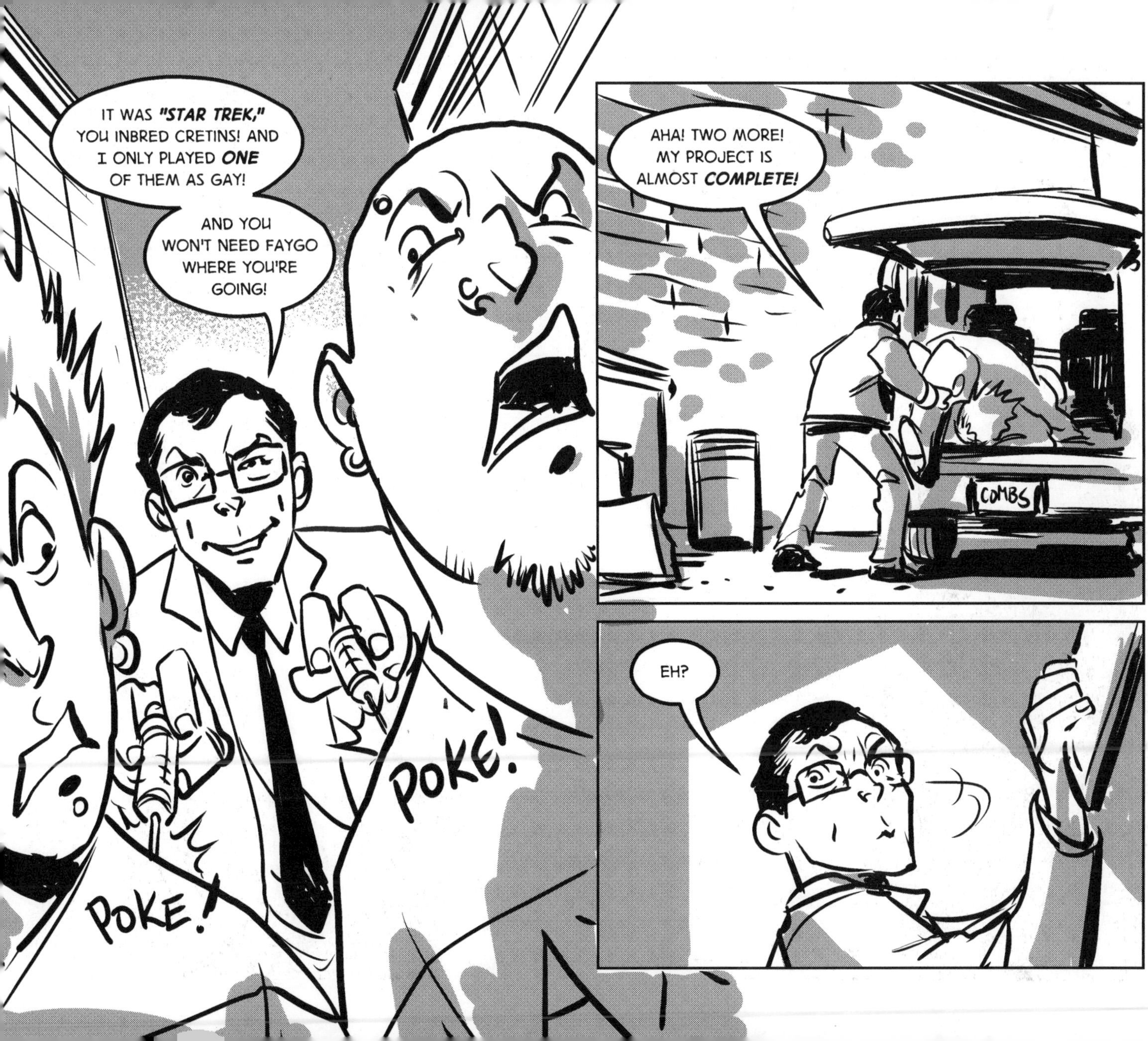
IT WAS "STAR TREK," YOU INBRED CRETINS! AND I ONLY PLAYED ONE OF THEM AS GAY!
AND YOU WON'T NEED FAYGO WHERE YOU'RE GOING!
POKE!
POKE!
AHA! TWO MORE! MY PROJECT IS ALMOST COMPLETE!
COMBS
EH?

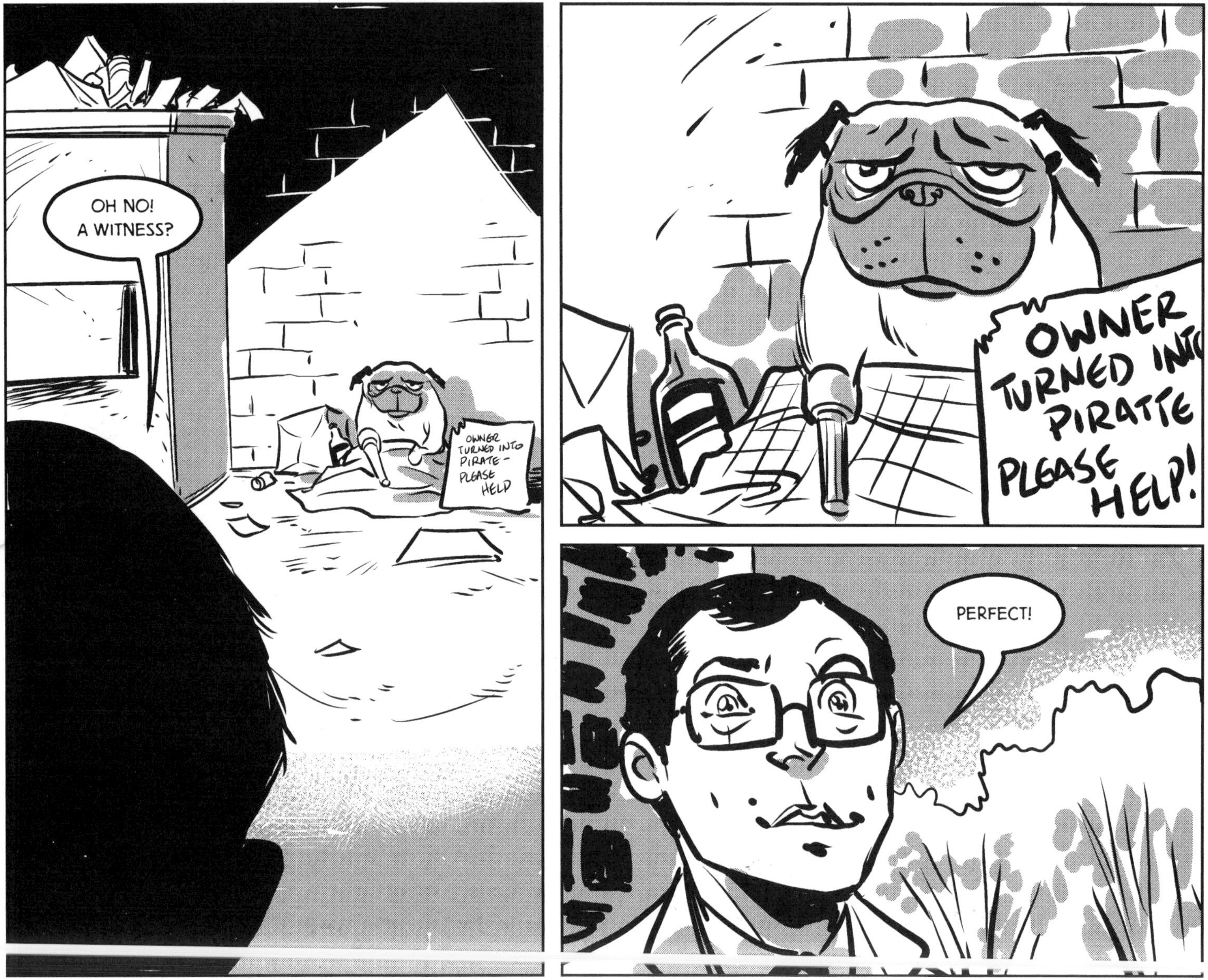
OH NO! A WITNESS?
OWNER TURNED INT PIRATTE PLEASE HELP!
PERFECT!

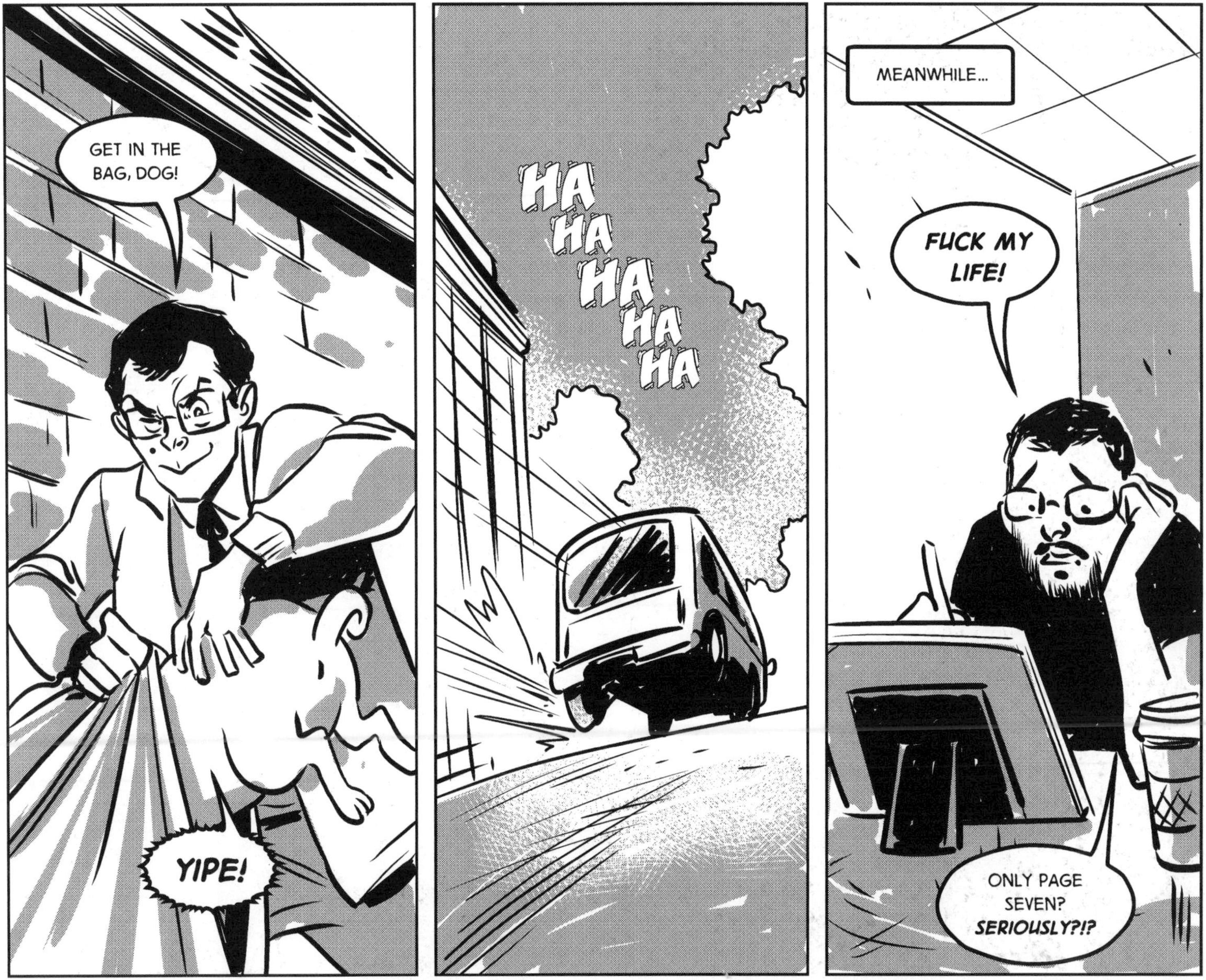

GET IN THE BAG, DOG!
YIPE!
HA HA HA HA HA
MEANWHILE...
FUCK MY LIFE!
ONLY PAGE SEVEN? SERIOUSLY?!?

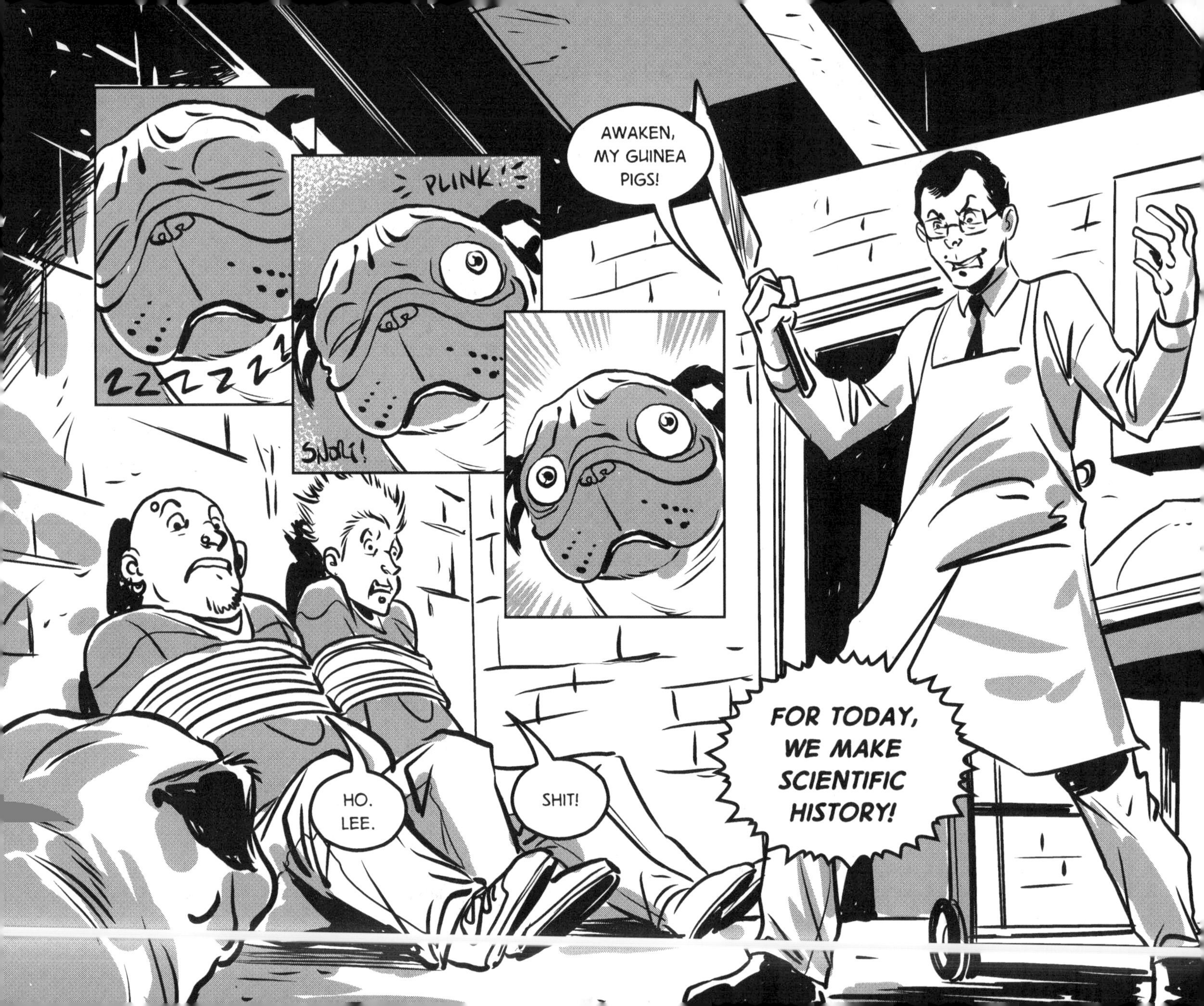
ZZZZZZZZ
PLINK!
SNORT!
AWAKEN, MY GUINEA PIGS!
FOR TODAY, WE MAKE SCIENTIFIC HISTORY!
HO. LEE.
SHIT!

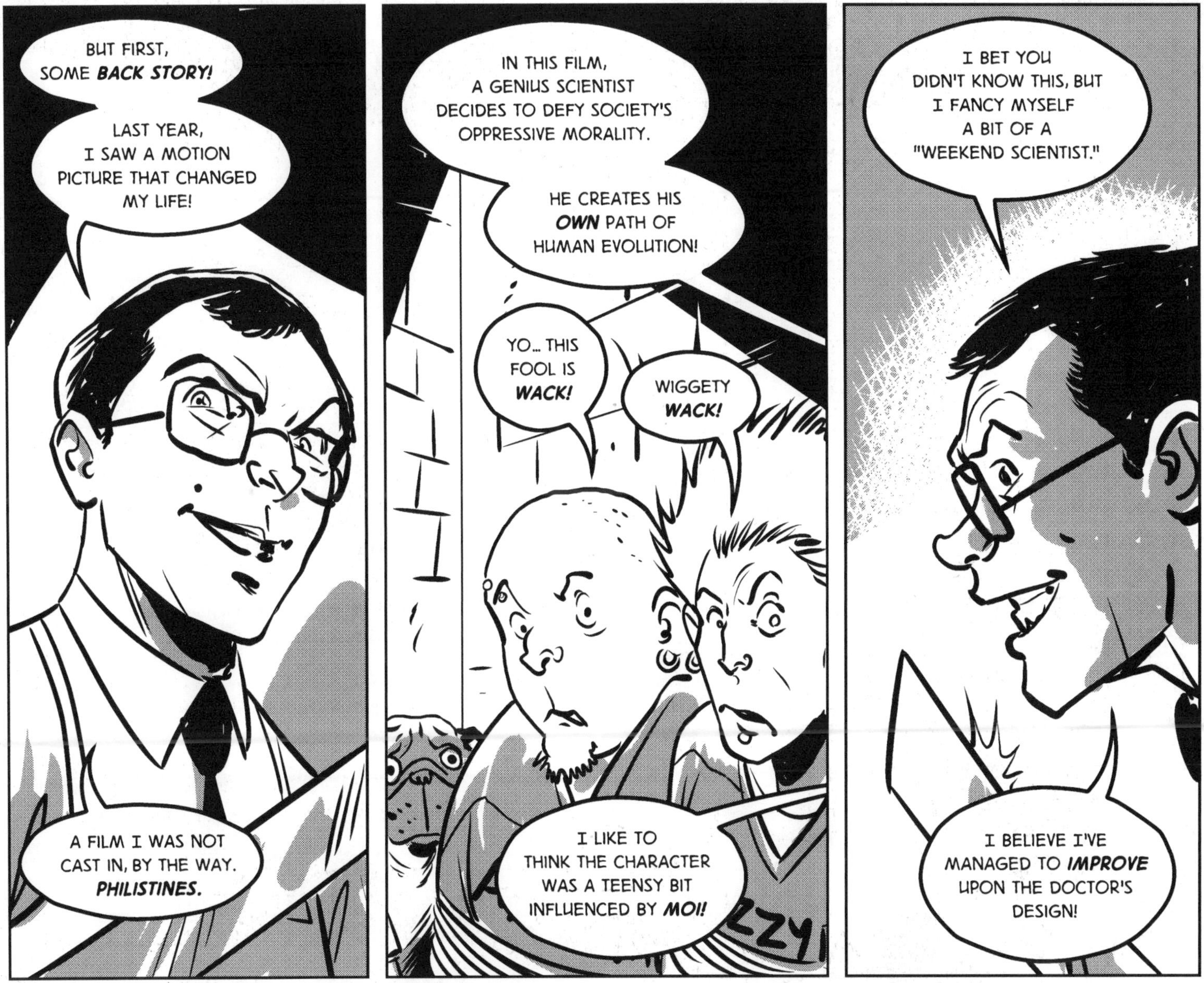
BUT FIRST, SOME BACK STORY!
LAST YEAR, I SAW A MOTION PICTURE THAT CHANGED MY LIFE!
A FILM I WAS NOT CAST IN, BY THE WAY. PHILISTINES.
IN THIS FILM, A GENIUS SCIENTIST DECIDES TO DEFY SOCIETY'S OPPRESSIVE MORALITY.
HE CREATES HIS OWN PATH OF HUMAN EVOLUTION!
YO... THIS FOOL IS WACK!
WIGGETY WACK!
I LIKE TO THINK THE CHARACTER WAS A TEENSY BIT INFLUENCED BY MOI!
I BET YOU DIDN'T KNOW THIS, BUT I FANCY MYSELF A BIT OF A "WEEKEND SCIENTIST."
I BELIEVE I'VE MANAGED TO IMPROVE UPON THE DOCTOR'S DESIGN!

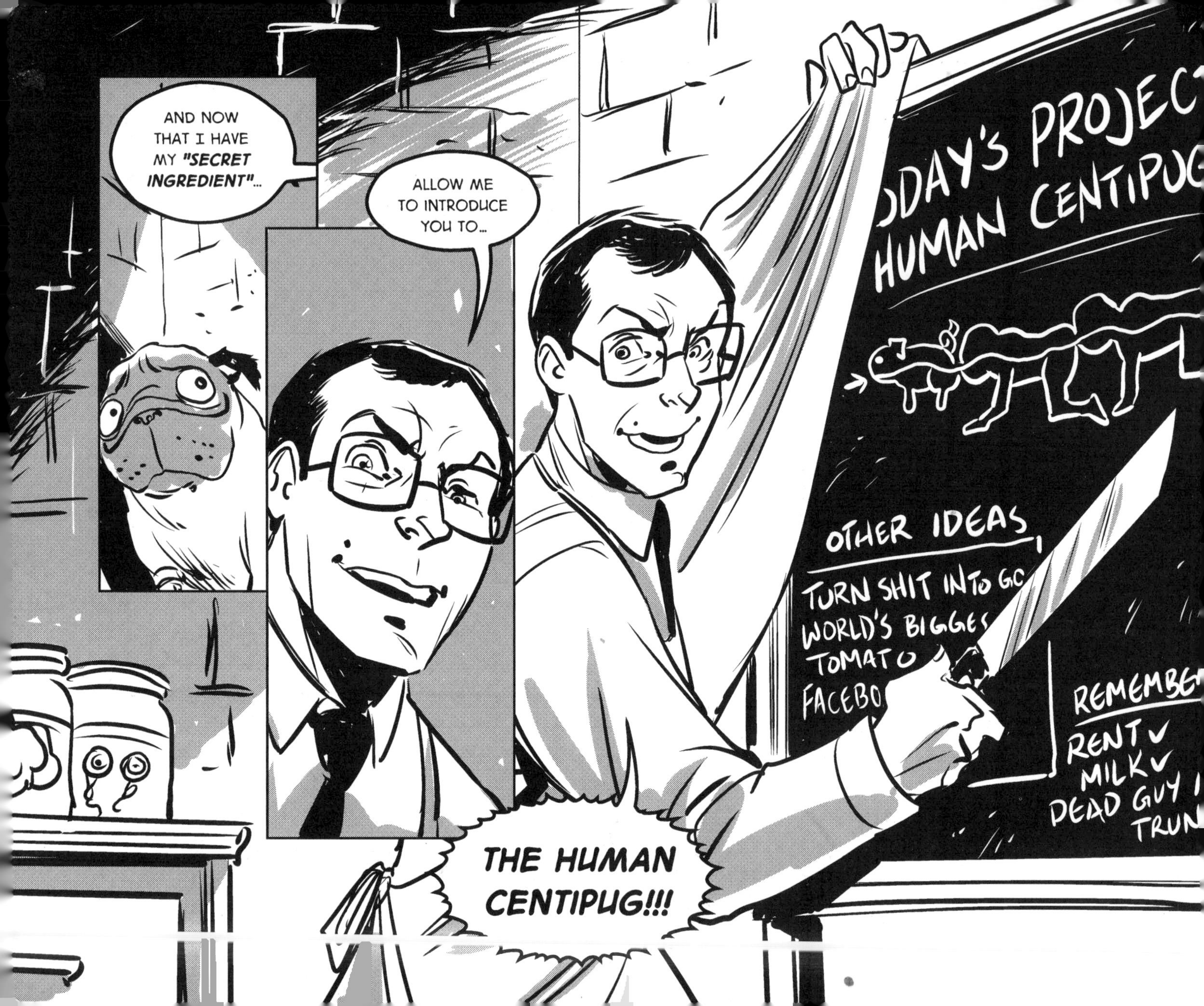
AND NOW THAT I HAVE MY "SECRET INGREDIENT"...
ALLOW ME TO INTRODUCE YOU TO...
ODAY'S PROJEC
HUMAN CENTIPUG
OTHER IDEAS
TURN SHIT INTO GC
WORLD'S BIGGES
TOMATO
FACEBO
REMEMBE
RENT✓
MILK✓
DEAD GUY I
TRUN
THE HUMAN CENTIPUG!!!

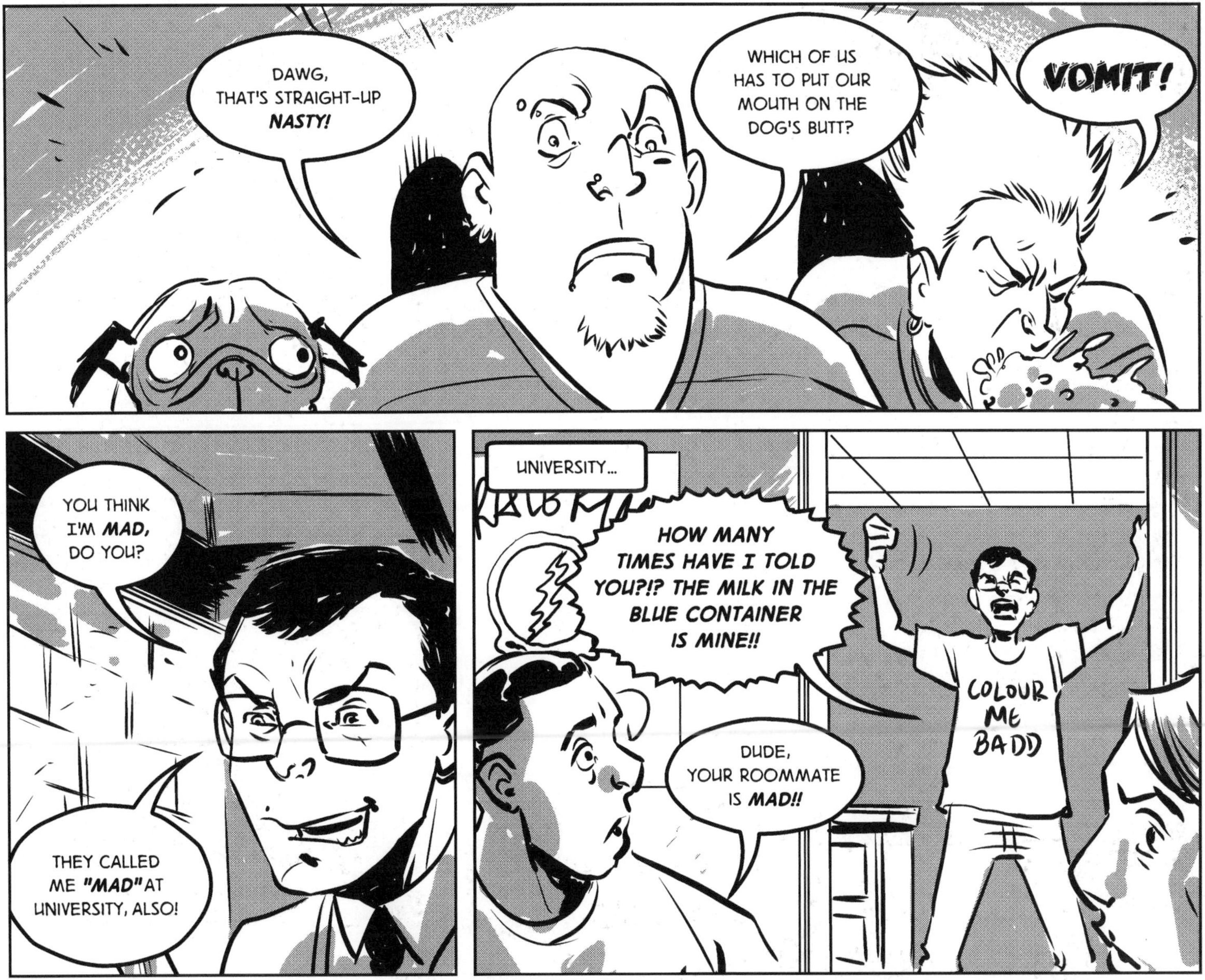
DAWG, THAT'S STRAIGHT-UP NASTY!
WHICH OF US HAS TO PUT OUR MOUTH ON THE DOG'S BUTT?
VOMIT!
YOU THINK I'M MAD, DO YOU?
THEY CALLED ME "MAD" AT UNIVERSITY, ALSO!
UNIVERSITY...
HOW MANY TIMES HAVE I TOLD YOU?!? THE MILK IN THE BLUE CONTAINER IS MINE!!
COLOUR ME BADD
DUDE, YOUR ROOMMATE IS MAD!!

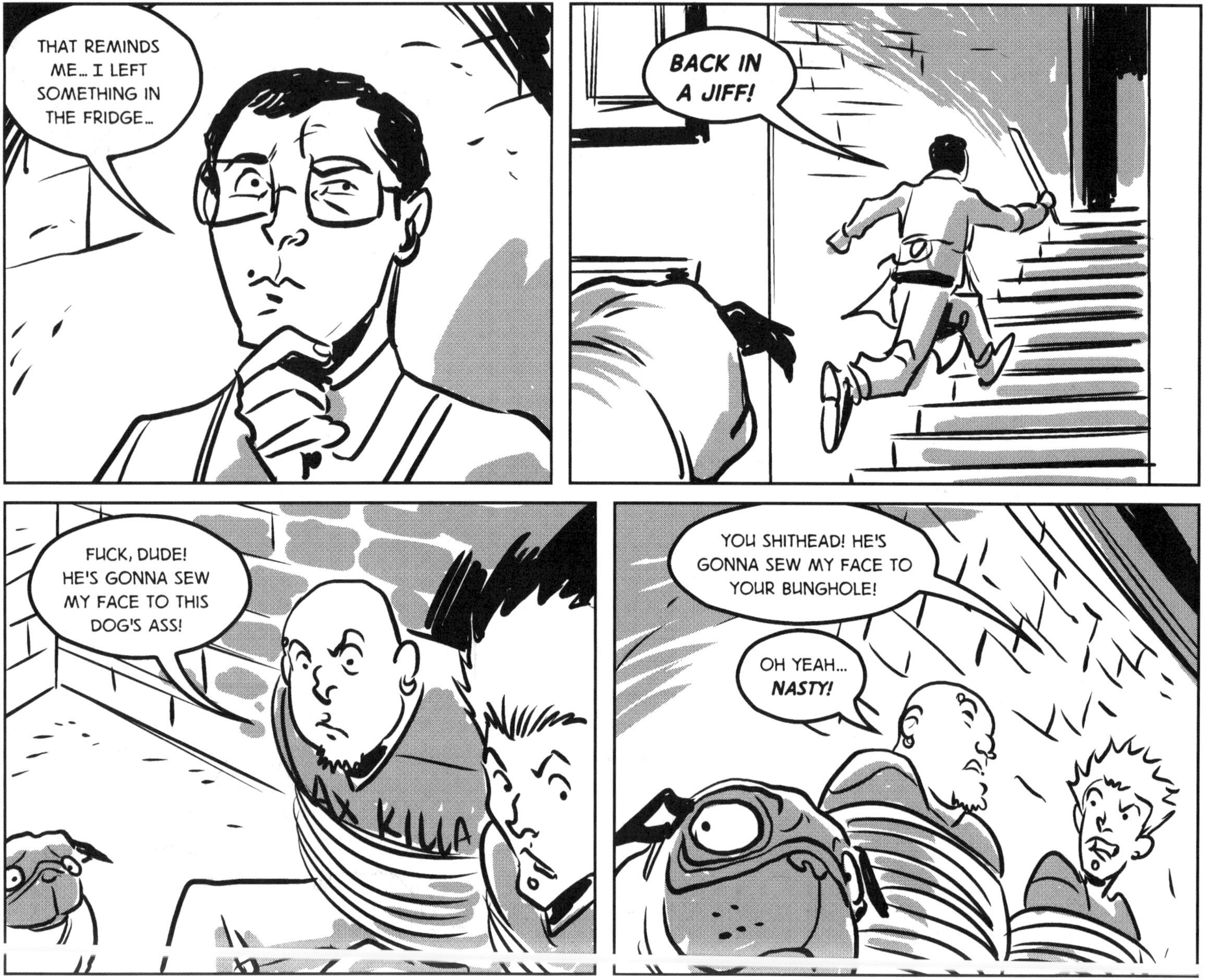
THAT REMINDS ME... I LEFT SOMETHING IN THE FRIDGE...
BACK IN A JIFF!
FUCK, DUDE! HE'S GONNA SEW MY FACE TO THIS DOG'S ASS!
AX KILLA
YOU SHITHEAD! HE'S GONNA SEW MY FACE TO YOUR BUNGHOLE!
OH YEAH... NASTY!

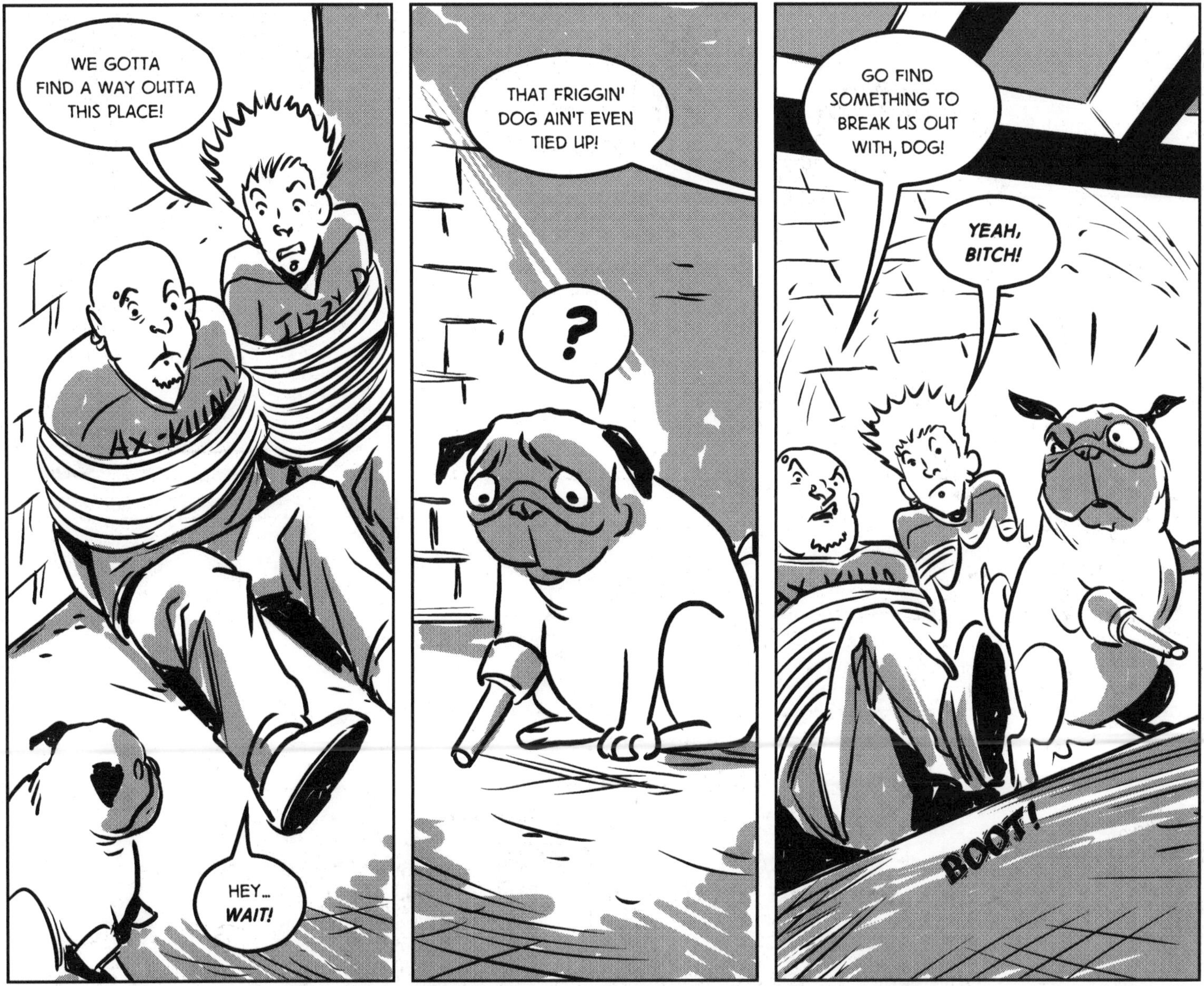
WE GOTTA FIND A WAY OUTTA THIS PLACE!
HEY... WAIT!
THAT FRIGGIN' DOG AIN'T EVEN TIED UP!
?
GO FIND SOMETHING TO BREAK US OUT WITH, DOG!
YEAH, BITCH!
BOOT!

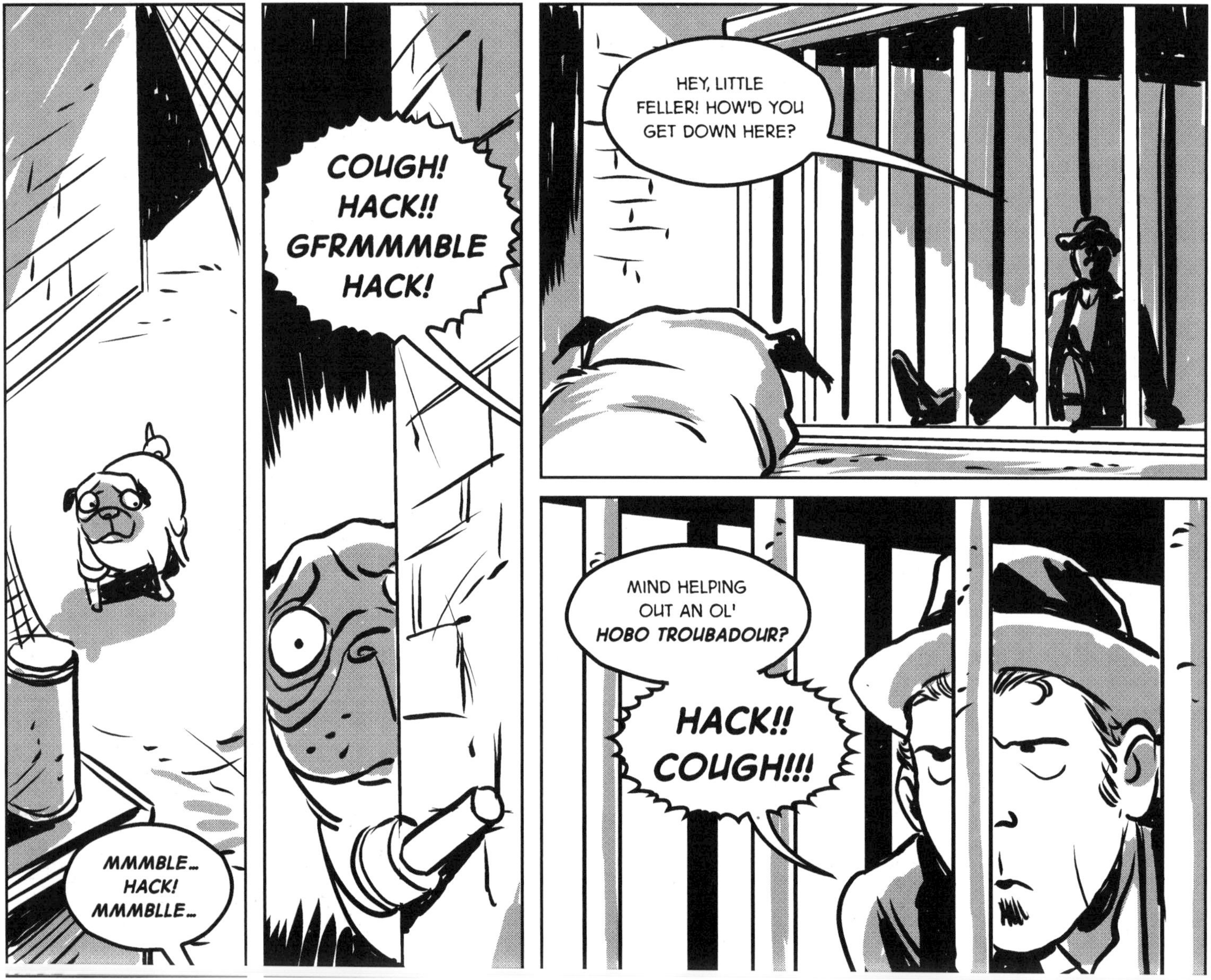
MMMBLE...
HACK!
MMMBLLE...
COUGH!
HACK!!
GFRMMMBLE
HACK!
HEY, LITTLE
FELLER! HOW'D YOU
GET DOWN HERE?
MIND HELPING
OUT AN OL'
HOBO TROUBADOUR?
HACK!!
COUGH!!!

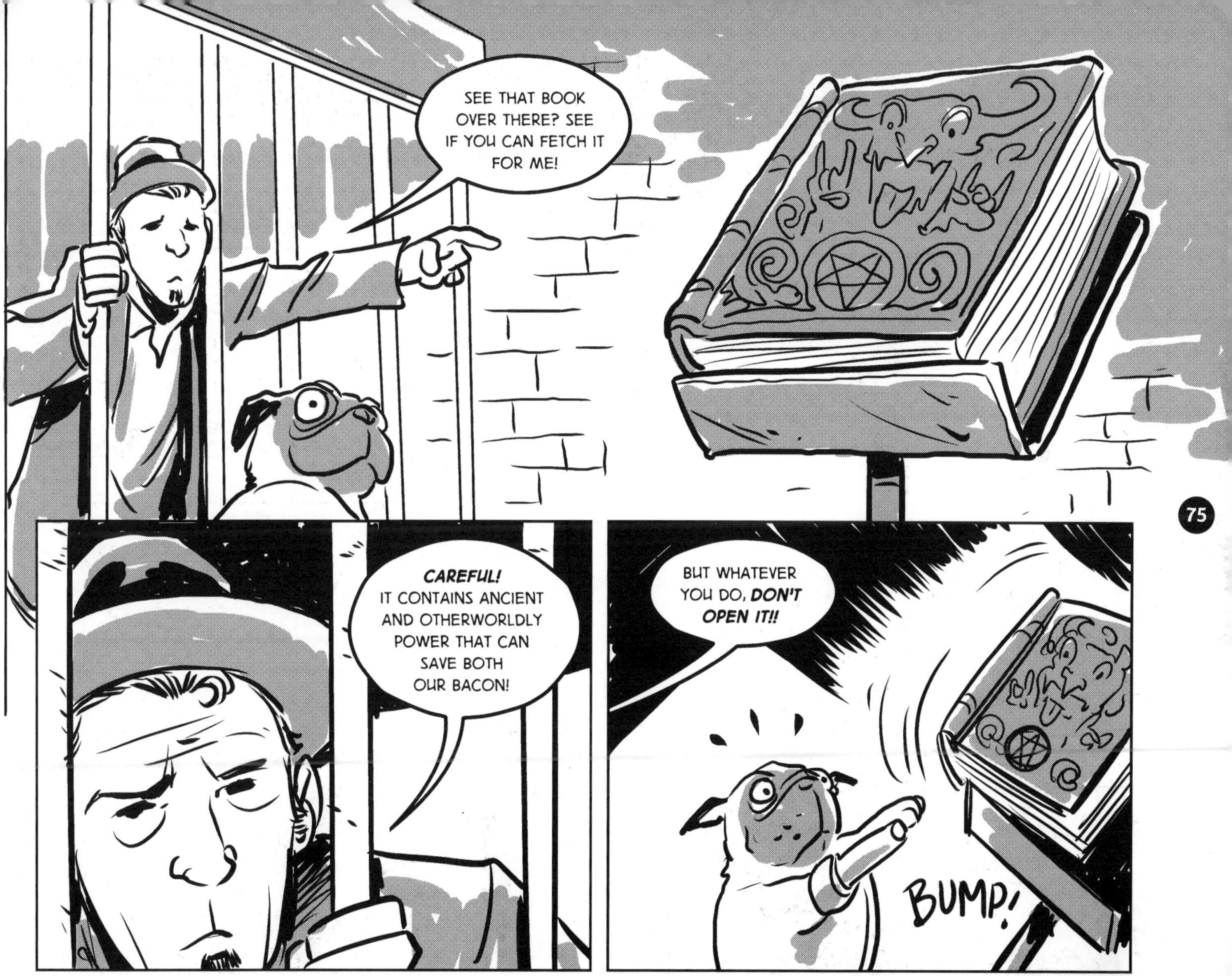
SEE THAT BOOK OVER THERE? SEE IF YOU CAN FETCH IT FOR ME!
CAREFUL! IT CONTAINS ANCIENT AND OTHERWORLDLY POWER THAT CAN SAVE BOTH OUR BACON!
BUT WHATEVER YOU DO, DON'T OPEN IT!!
BUMP!

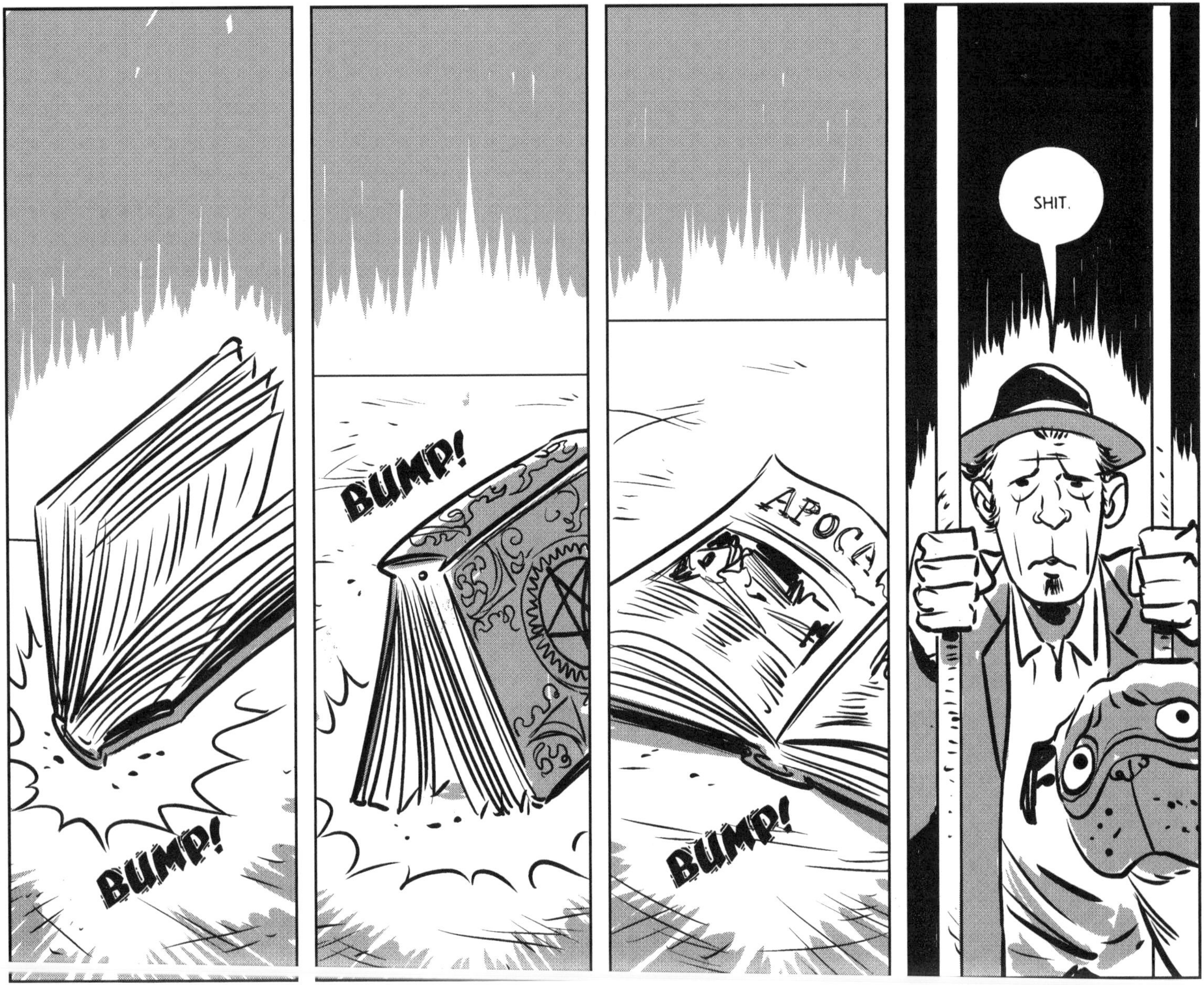
BUMP!
BUMP!
APOCA
BUMP!
SHIT.

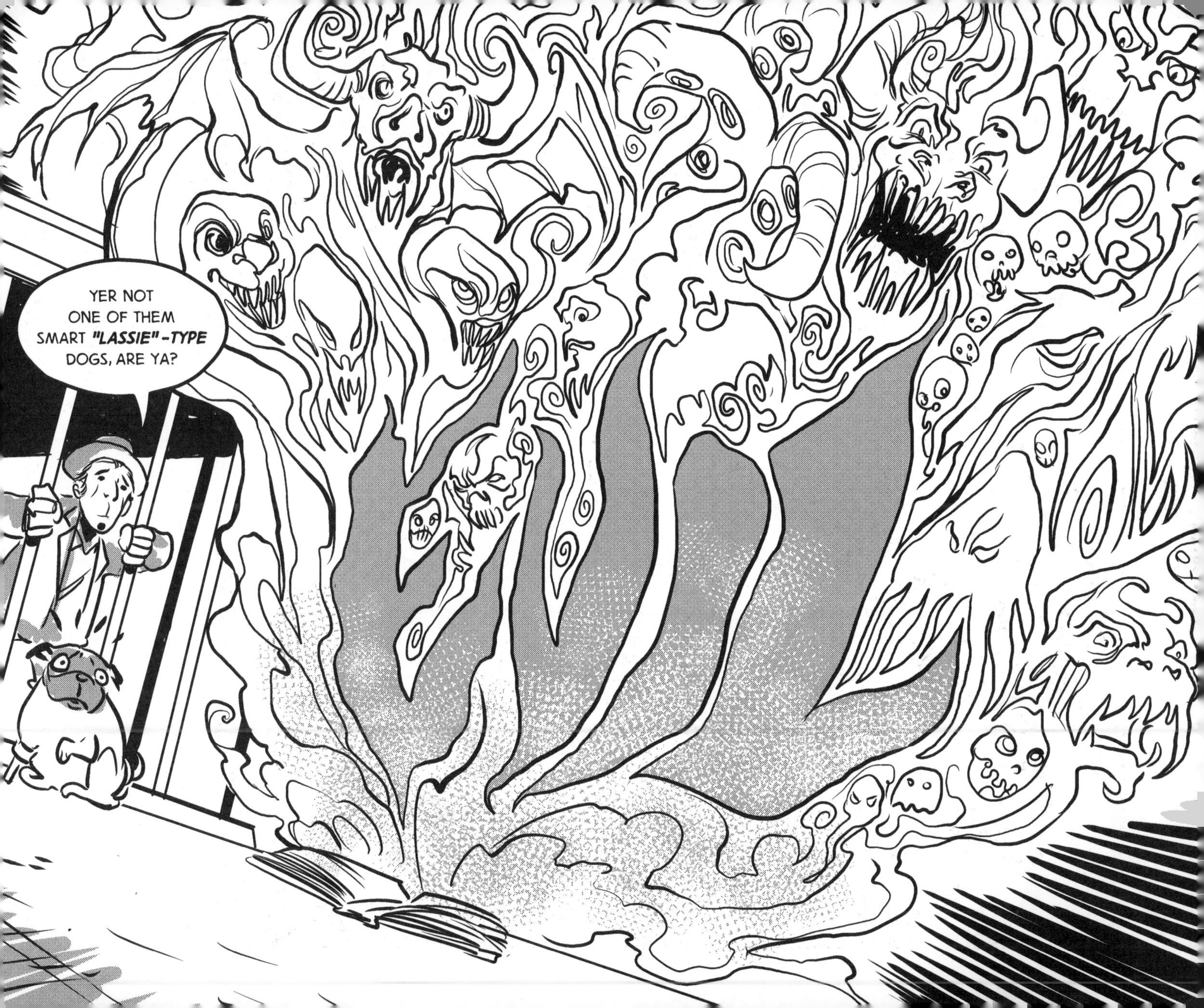
YER NOT ONE OF THEM SMART "LASSIE"-TYPE DOGS, ARE YA?

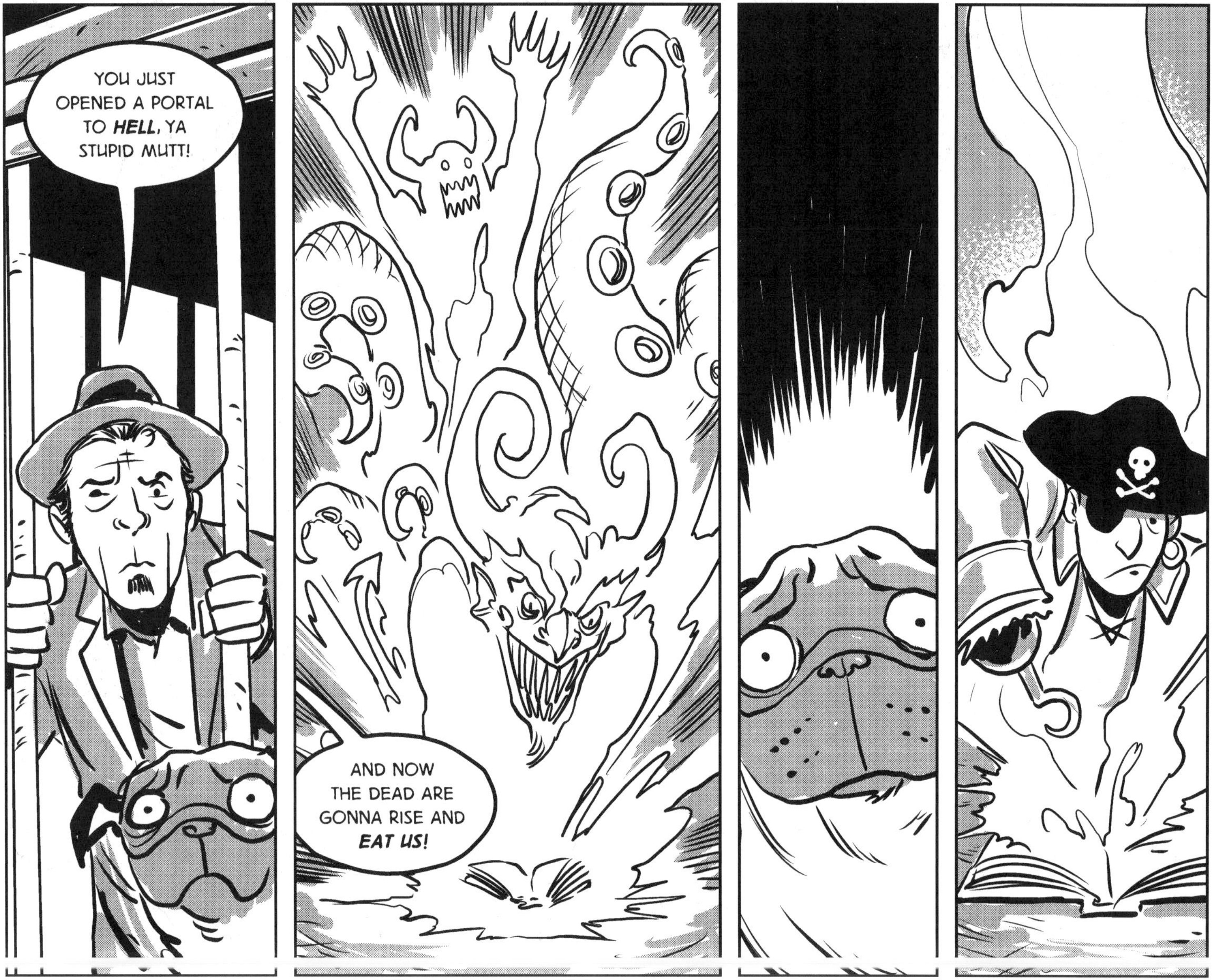
YOU JUST OPENED A PORTAL TO **HELL**, YA STUPID MUTT!
AND NOW THE DEAD ARE GONNA RISE AND ***EAT US!***

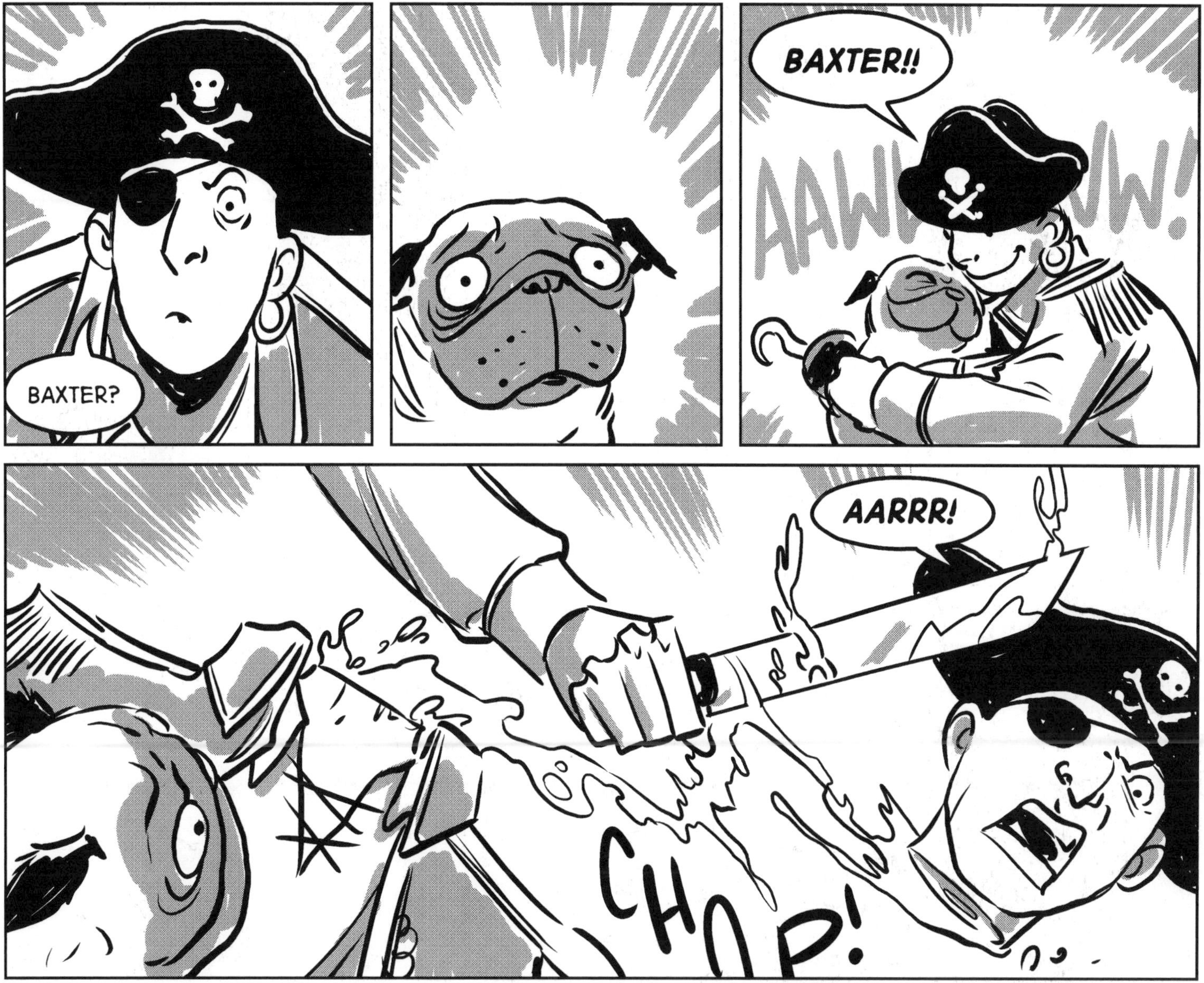
BAXTER?
BAXTER!!
AARRR!
CHOP!

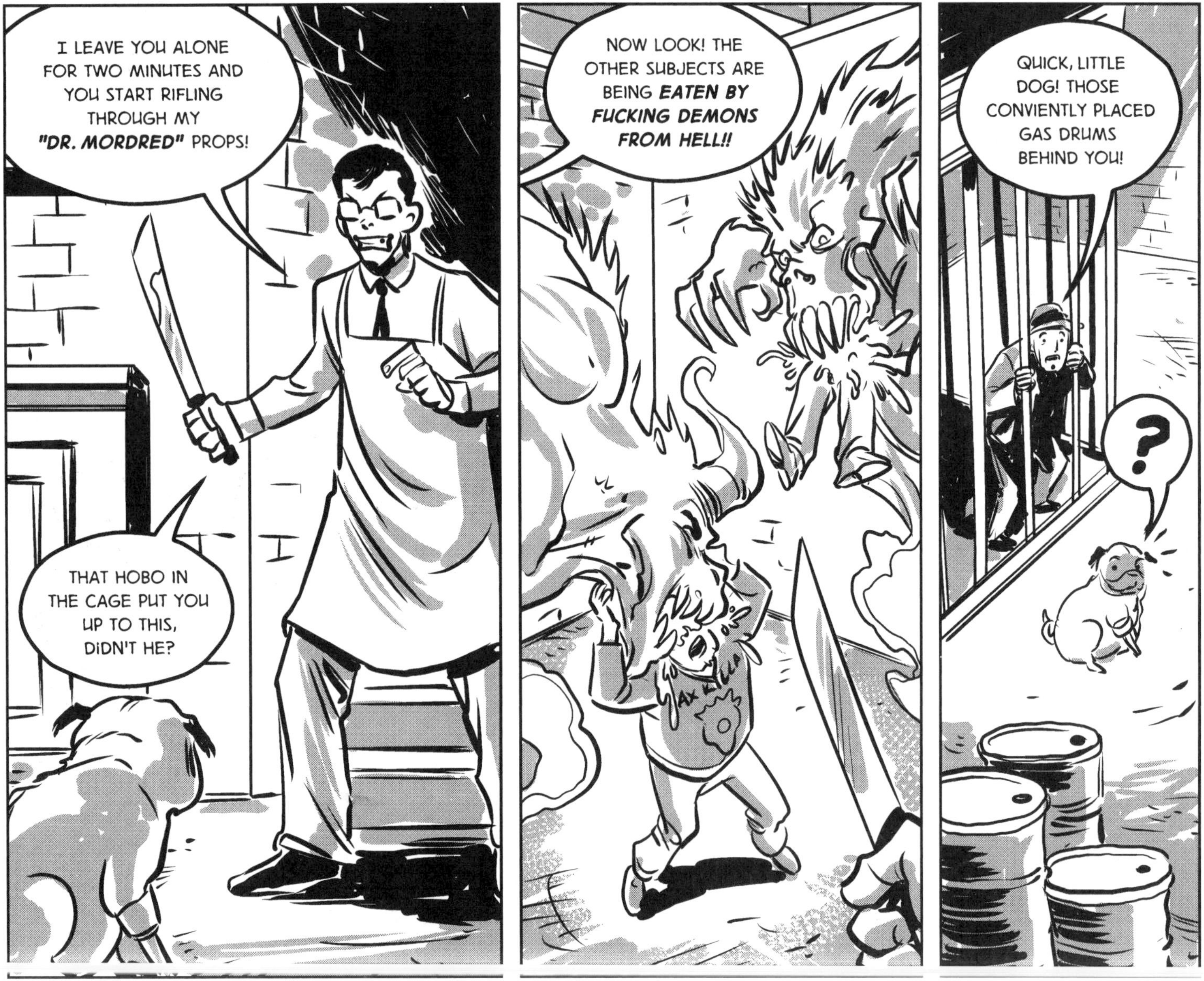
I LEAVE YOU ALONE FOR TWO MINUTES AND YOU START RIFLING THROUGH MY **"DR. MORDRED"** PROPS!
THAT HOBO IN THE CAGE PUT YOU UP TO THIS, DIDN'T HE?
NOW LOOK! THE OTHER SUBJECTS ARE BEING **EATEN BY FUCKING DEMONS FROM HELL!!**
QUICK, LITTLE DOG! THOSE CONVIENTLY PLACED GAS DRUMS BEHIND YOU!
?

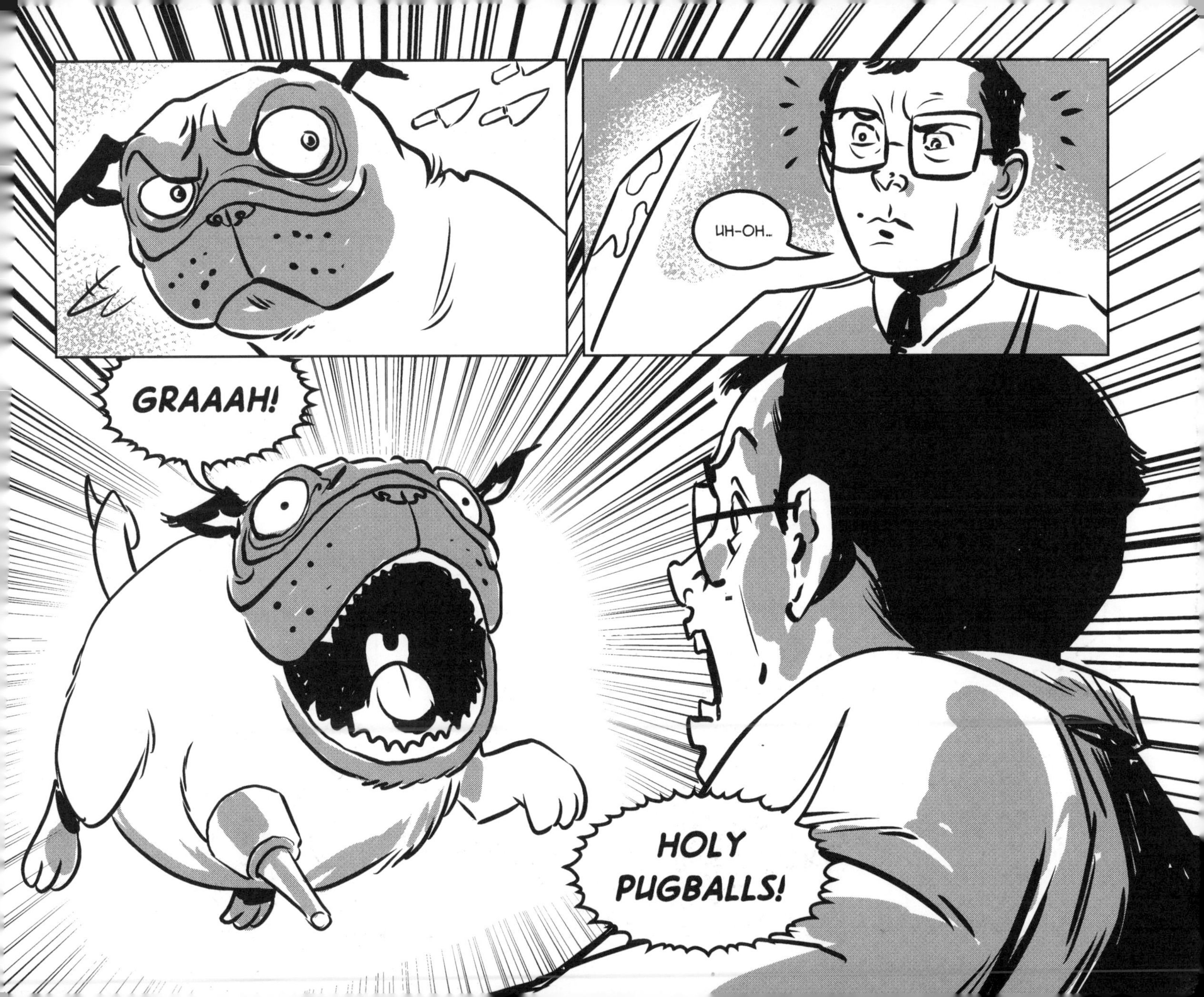
UH-OH...
GRAAAH!
HOLY PUGBALLS!

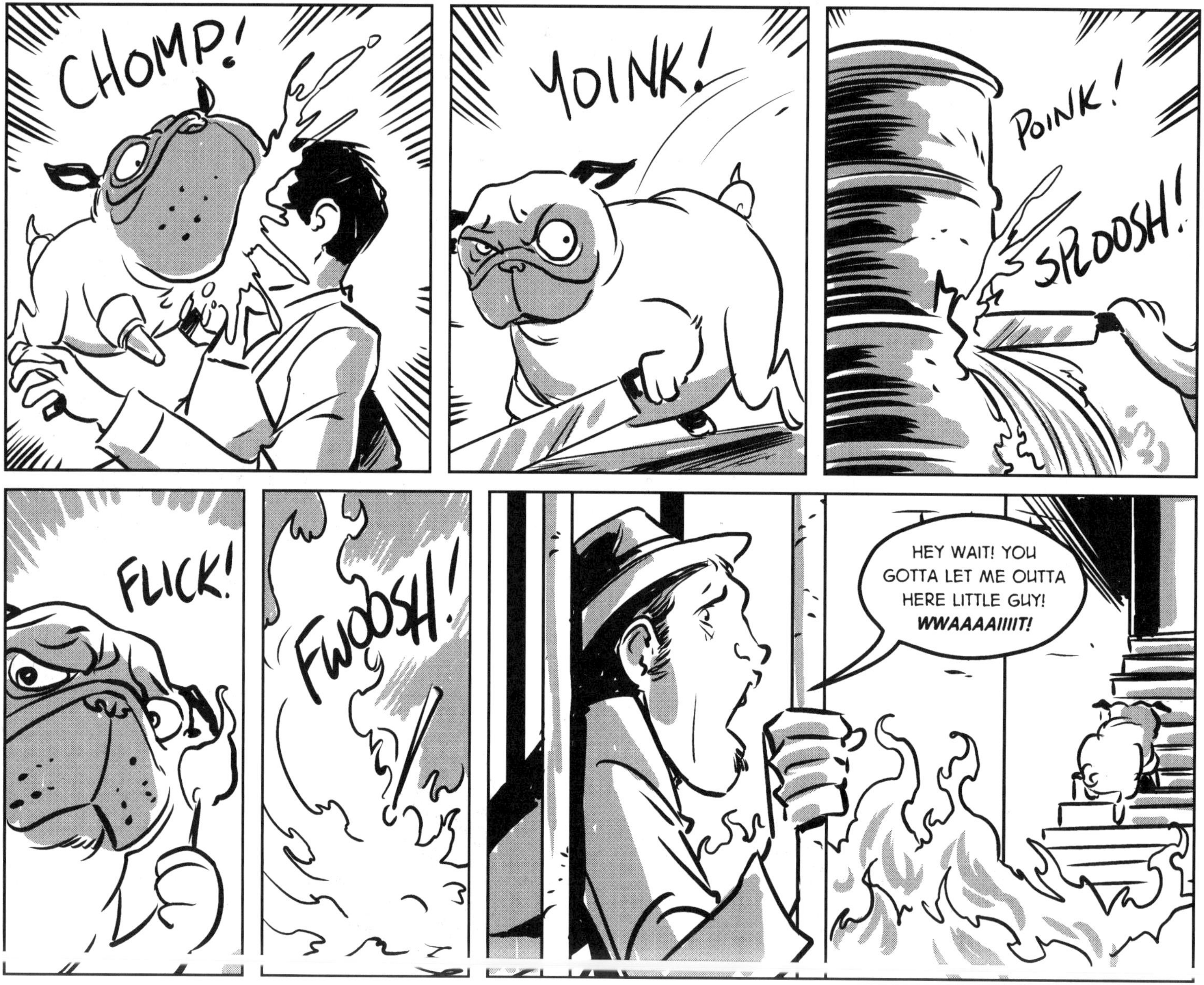
CHOMP!
YOINK!
POINK!
SPLOOSH!
FLICK!
FWOOSH!
HEY WAIT! YOU GOTTA LET ME OUTTA HERE LITTLE GUY! WWAAAAIIIIT!

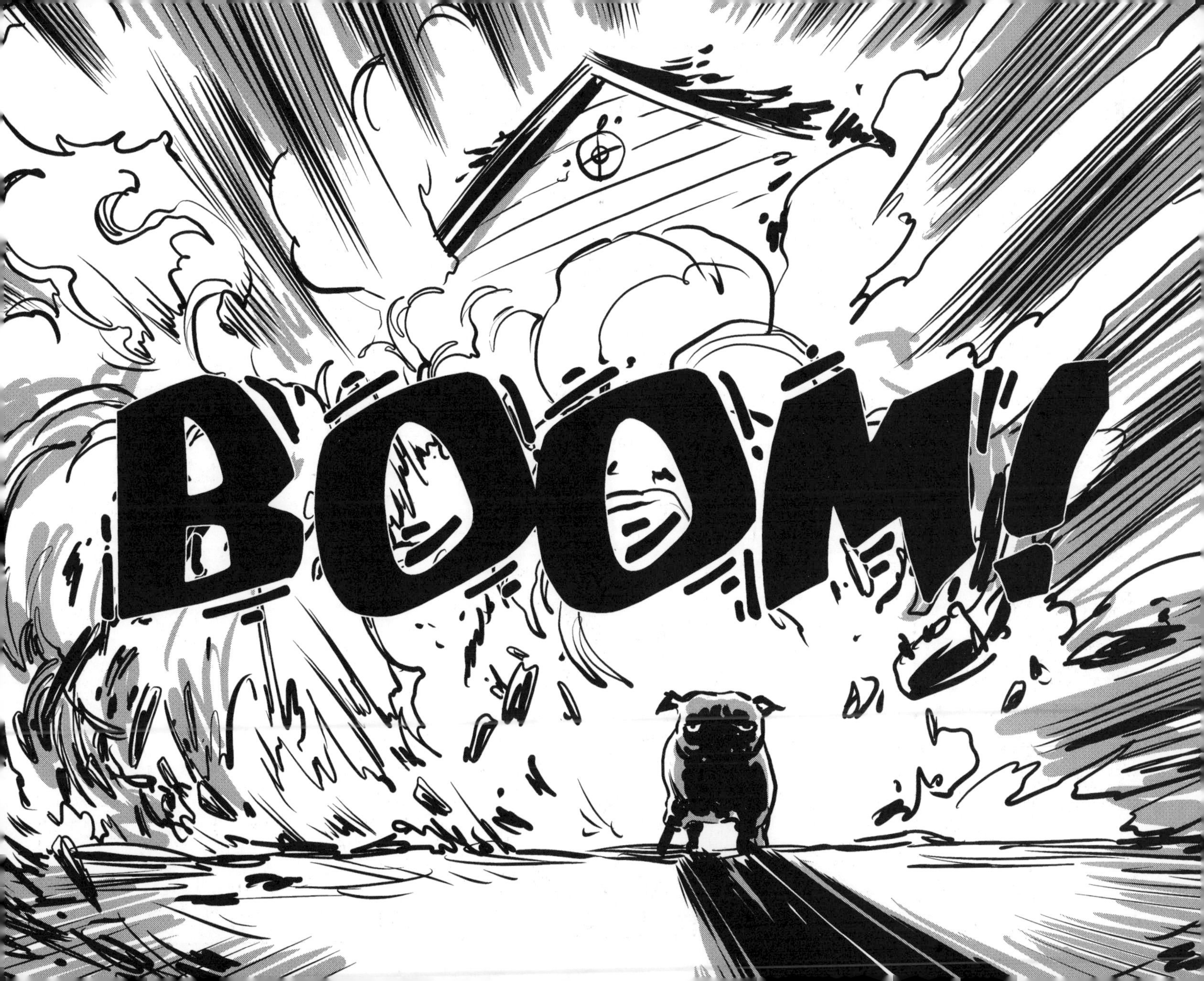
BOOM!!

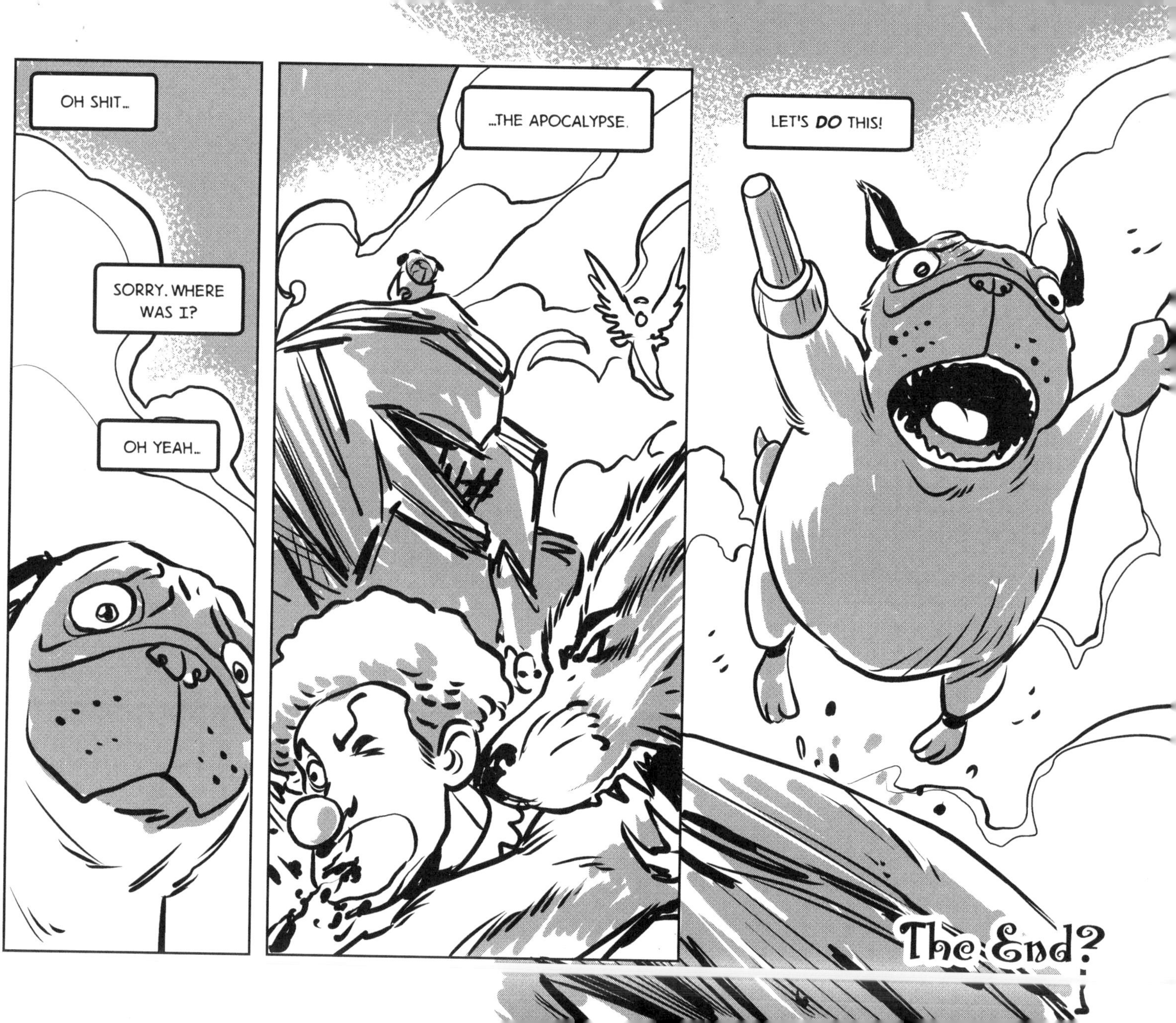
OH SHIT...
SORRY. WHERE WAS I?
OH YEAH...
...THE APOCALYPSE.
LET'S **DO** THIS!
The End?

MIKE NORTON has been working in comics for over ten years. He's made a name for himself working on books like *Queen & Country*, *Gravity*, *Runaways*, *All-New Atom*, *Green Arrow/Black Canary*, *Billy Batson & The Magic of Shazam*, and *Young Justice*. He is currently drawing his own series, *Revival* and the weekly webcomic, *Battlepug*.

He is also very, very tall.

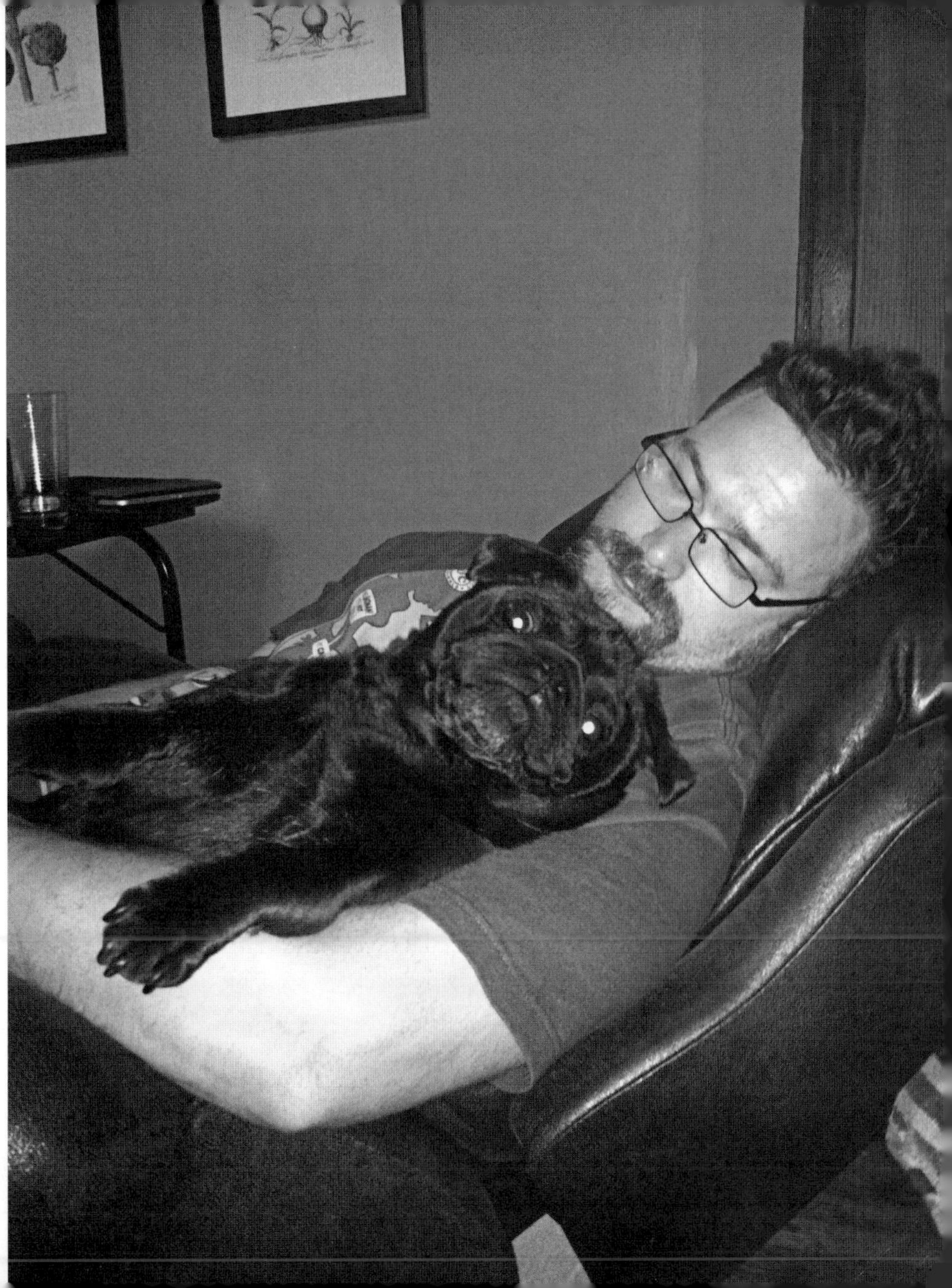

OTHER BOOKS AVAILABLE FROM ONI PRESS...

THE BIG BOOK OF
BARRY
WEEN
BOY GENIUS
JUDD WINICK

THE BIG BOOK OF BARRY WEEN, BOY GENIUS
By Judd Winick
360 Pages • 6"x9" TPB, B&W
ISBN 978-1-934964-02-6

RICK SPEARS
CHUCK BB
BLACK METAL
BOOK ONE

BLACK METAL, VOLUME 1: THE GRIM RETURN
By Rick Spears & Chuck BB
160 Pages, Digest, B&W
ISBN 978-1-932664-72-0

blue monday

BLUE MONDAY, VOLUME 1: THE KIDS ARE ALRIGHT
By Chynna Clugston
136 Pages, Digest, B&W
ISBN 978-1-929998-62-3

Courtney
Volume One
Crumrin
The Night Things
Ted Naifeh

COURTNEY CRUMRIN, VOLUME 1: THE NIGHT THINGS HC
By Ted Naifeh
144 Pages, Hardcover, Color
ISBN 978-1-934964-77-4

HOPELESS
SAVAGES
GREATEST HITS
2000-2010

HOPELESS SAVAGES: GREATEST HITS
By Jen Van Meter and others
364 Pages, 6"x9" TPB, B&W
ISBN 978-1-934964-48-4

BRIAN WOOD • RYAN KELLY
LOCAL

LOCAL - DELUXE HARDCOVER
By Brian Wood & Ryan Kelly
384 Pages, Hardcover, B&W
ISBN 978-1-934964-00-2

THE SIXTH GUN
CULLEN BUNN
BRIAN HURTT

THE SIXTH GUN, VOLUME 1: COLD DEAD FINGERS
By Cullen Bunn, Brian Hurtt, Bill Crabtree
176 Pages, TPB, Color
ISBN 978-1-934964-60-6

SPELL
CHECKERS
Volume 1

SPELL CHECKERS, VOLUME 1
By Jamie S. Rich, Nicolas Hitori De, Joëlle Jones
152 Pages, Digest, B&W
ISBN 978-1-934964-32-3

ONI PRESS
REVOLUTIONIZE COMICS

AVAILABLE AT FINER COMIC SHOPS EVERYWHERE.
FOR A COMICS STORE NEAR YOU, CALL 1-888-COMIC-BOOK OR VISIT WWW.COMICSHOPS.US.

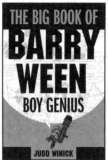

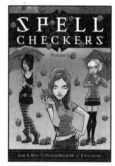